Meditation
as
Contemplative Inquiry

Meditation
as
Contemplative Inquiry

When Knowing Becomes Love

Arthur Zajonc

LINDISFARNE BOOKS
2009

LINDISFARNE BOOKS
An imprint of SteinerBooks/Anthroposophic Press, Inc.
610 Main Street, Great Barrington, Massachusetts 01230
www.lindisfarne.org www.steinerbooks.org

Grateful acknowledgment is made to the publishers to reprint the following
previously published material:

Juan Ramón Jiménez, "I am not I" in *The Winged Energy of Delight*, trans. Robert
Bly, published by Harper Perennial, NY, 2005.

Rumi, "The Guest House" in Rumi: The Book of Love, trans. Coleman Barks,
published by HarperCollins, New York, 2003.

Rumi, from The Essential Rumi, trans. Coleman Barks with John Moyne,
Harper San Francisco, 1995.

Leopold Staff, "Foundations" in Postwar *Polish Poetry*, ed. and trans. Czeslaw
Milosz, published by Bantam, Doubleday, Dell, New York, 1965.

T.S. Eliot, "Four Quartets: East Coker III" in *The Complete Poems and Plays*,
published by Harcourt, Brace and World, New York, 1962.

Theodor Schwenk, plate 25: the formation of a train of vortices in water by
the author, *Sensitive Chaos: The Creation of Flowing Forms in Water and Air*, revised
edition, published by Rudolf Steiner Press, Forest Row, UK, 1996.

LIBRARY OF CONGRESS CATALOGING-IN-PUBLICATION DATA

Zajonc, Arthur.
 Meditation as contemplative inquiry : when knowing becomes love / Arthur
Zajonc.
 p. cm.
 ISBN 978-1-58420-062-8
 1. Meditation. 2. Contemplation. I. Title.
 BL627.Z35 2008
 204'.35–dc22

2008037447

Printed in the United States

FOR HEIDE

Contents

Introduction

We must learn to reawaken

and keep ourselves awake, not

by mechanical aids, but by an

infinite expectation of the dawn,

which does not forsake us

in our soundest sleep.

— HENRY DAVID THOREAU

Being Awake, Fostering Peace

In his remarkable record of two years at Walden Pond, Thoreau wrote of the morning: "Little is to be expected of that day, if it can be called a day, to which we are not awakened by our Genius, but by the mechanical nudgings of some servitor, are not awakened by our own newly acquired force and aspirations from within, instead of factory bells ....The millions are awake enough for physical labor; but only one in a million is awake enough for effective intellectual exertion, only one in a hundred millions to a poetic or divine life. To be awake is to be alive. I have never yet met a man who was quite awake. How could I have looked him in the face?"[1]

---

1. Henry David Thoreau, *Walden and Civil Disobedience*, edited by Owen Thomas, (NY: Norton Critical Edition, 1966) pp. 60-61.

Yes, to be awake is to be truly alive. Yet how, in the face of fear, doubt, and deadening routine, can we awaken ourselves to a "poetic and divine life"? If not by "factory bells" or other external means, then by what? Thoreau pointed to our genius, that high principle in each of us, as the force that can awaken. Our genius lives in expectation of the unknown as we expect the new day. It prompts us to be awake to the subtle dimensions of experience, to meet the sufferings and joys of life with equanimity, and to sense the unknown that continually invites us after her. How can we come into more regular and sustained contact with our genius?

Upon meeting someone more awake than I, I have felt the conflicting emotions of hesitation and eagerness, of resentment, excitement, and longing to become more like them, more present and more alive. The timeless story of the Buddha captures the feeling of such an encounter.[2] It is said that soon after his enlightenment, the Buddha passed a man on the road who was struck by his extraordinary presence. The man stopped and asked,

"My friend, what are you? Are you a celestial being or a god?"
"No," said the Buddha.
"Well, then, are you some kind of magician or wizard?"
Again the Buddha answered, "No."
"Are you a man?"
"No."
"Well, my friend, what then are you?"
The Buddha replied, "I am awake."

The name Buddha means "one who is awake."

Together with wakefulness, the Buddha is said to have radiated peacefulness. Wakefulness requires peace as its complement. In other words, if one is to be more fully awake, then the burdens of such wakefulness require a steadiness of mind, a largeness of heart, and a deep equanimity in the face of new and significant experiences. I think of Nelson Mandela or Rigoberta Menchu Tum confronting the suffering of their friends and people with open eyes and open hearts, not turning away from the

---

2. Joseph Goldstein and Jack Kornfield, *Seeking the Heart of Wisdom* (Boston: Shambhala, 2001), p. 3.

suffering but turning toward it. They were awake to the suffering not only of themselves but of their entire communities. Both have become exemplars because they met suffering with compassion, and because together with truth they sought reconciliation instead of revenge.

To see is to suffer sorrow as well as to experience joy, and the more fully we see the greater must be our peace of heart in order to carry what is lived. I sometimes imagine to myself that, like the metalworker who pours molten metal into a crucible, life pours its experience into the pliant, refractory vessel of the wakeful heart. The heat of truth softens and molds us according to its own laws, if we have the patience and strength to endure it. Simone Weil put it well when she wrote, "To love truth means to endure the void and, as a result, to accept death. Truth is on the side of death."[3] Something dies in us every time we change. To make space for the true, familiar well-worn habits must give way.

Personal Practice and Finding Fellowship

One well-established way of cultivating wakefulness and peace is contemplative practice. I began my own practice of meditation over thirty-five years ago, at about the same time I started my serious study of physics. Since that time, contemplative practice has been a necessary part of my life, including my work as a scientist. Yet for many years I felt alone in my stubborn conjunction of the scientific and the contemplative. Occasionally I would find a colleague and companion who also combined contemplative striving with a vigorous scholarly life, most commonly a humanist or artist. But this situation is changing.

By now it has become clear that contemplative practice works. The hundreds of scientific studies of its efficacy have shown the value of meditation in many health contexts. A high point for me in this regard was a large conference at MIT in 2003 that I co-facilitated, called "Investigating the Mind."[4] A distinguished group of Buddhist scholars and monks,

---

3. Simone Weil, *Gravity and Grace*, trans. E. Crawford and M. von der Ruhr (New York: Routledge, 2002), p. 11.
4. Anne Harrington and Arthur Zajonc, *The Dalai Lama at MIT*, (Cambridge, MA: Harvard University Press, 2006)

including the Dalai Lama, were on stage with an equally distinguished group of cognitive scientists and psychologists. Richard Davidson from the University of Wisconsin in Madison was presenting data from his extensive studies of eight expert Buddhist contemplatives during long periods of meditation.[5] His research was meticulous, with every control one could imagine to eliminate experimental artifacts. The data were compelling. Even at the level of neurophysiology, dramatic changes were evident, and these went far beyond what one could expect from any normal variations.

As powerful as Davidson's presentation was, it only confirmed what thousands of years of personal experience all over the world had already affirmed. Meditation matters. It matters not only to monks but also to patients at the Center for Mindfulness at the University of Massachusetts Medical School and 250 similar centers around the world. It matters to hundreds of thousands of students in colleges and universities who each semester are benefiting from a pedagogy that has been enriched by the inclusion of contemplative practices.[6] The health, educational, business, and personal benefits of meditation are now well documented and widely appreciated by millions of Americans and uncounted others around the world.

This was brought home to me when I was a program director for the Fetzer Institute, and the president of the Nathan Cummings Foundation, Charles Halpern, suggested to me and others that perhaps it was time to inaugurate a "contemplative practice fellowship" program. I was certain no one would apply, beyond at most a handful of students or professors from religious or alternative colleges. Charlie persisted and even convinced the revered American Council of Learned Societies to administer the fellow-ships. The response to that first year's program in 1997 was tremendously positive; as I read the proposals I was delighted by their thoughtfulness and

5. Antoine Lutz, Lawrence L. Greischar, Nancy B. Rawlings, Matthieu Ricard, and Richard Davidson, *Proceeding of the National Academy of Sciences*, vol. 101, (Nov. 16, 2004), pp. 16369-16373.

6. *Teachers College Record*, Special Issue: "Contemplative Practices and Education," vol. 108 (September 2006), and www.contemplativemind.org, Academic Program of the Center for Contemplative Mind in Society.

variety. Between 1997 and 2007 more than 120 contemplative practice fellowships were awarded to a remarkable range of scholars each of whom has in some manner integrated contemplative practice into his or her university teaching. They come from distinguished colleges and universities throughout North America. In the first year alone they taught at places like Bryn Mawr (English), City University of New York (English), Suffolk University (law), University of Massachusetts (American studies), Colgate University (religion), Haverford College (philosophy), Clark University (English), Columbia University (education), University of Colorado (sociology), University of Michigan (music), University of Colorado, Denver (architecture), and University of California, Irvine (psychiatry).

Since 1997 there have been regional and national conferences on the theme of contemplation in higher education by many groups such as the Association of American Colleges and Universities, as well as at Columbia University, Amherst College, and the University of Michigan. The Higher Education Research Institute at UCLA has launched a Spirituality in Higher Education survey project. In my own Five College area we have had an official Five College Faculty Seminar on New Epistemologies and Contemplation for several years with over seventy participants, and among the Five Colleges some thirty-five courses are offered that include meditation in some form. The Center for Contemplative Mind in Society has been a crucial organization, helping to foster contemplative practice among not only academics but also social justice activists, lawyers, youth, environmental leaders, and other groups. I don't feel alone anymore, but I do feel that we are still at the very beginning. The invaluable contribution that meditation can make to all aspects of our lives, including learning and research, has only begun to be developed and appreciated.

Contemporary Contemplative Inquiry

I agree with those who have maintained that the true goal of contemplative practice, indeed of life, is the joining of insight and compassion, wisdom and love. To accomplish this requires that we find deep peace within and learn to be ever more awake, and thereby be of greater benefit in all we undertake. Our time is beset by problems: environmental problems, social justice issues, homelessness, health disasters, inequities in education, hunger, and poverty. These all require real-world solutions. Yet together with our tireless outer efforts, a comparable effort is needed to change who we are, to become, as Gandhi said, the solutions we envision for the world. We will need to find the means to engage in an inner work commensurate with our outer work.

The medieval European worldview recognized two orientations to life. One was termed *vita activa* and the other *vita contemplativa*, the active life and the contemplative life. Most of medieval society was given to the life of production, whether agriculture, handcrafts, the arts of war, or governance. In the monasteries, by contrast, the few were given to a life of prayer and contemplation, to *vita contemplativa*. While the monks did labor in the monastery gardens and kitchens to provide for themselves, the monastery walls protected them from the turmoil of the active life. Even work itself became a form of prayer for the medieval monk. *Laborare est orare*, they said: "to work is to pray."

The times are different now in that those who wish to live the contemplative life must simultaneously live the active life. No monastery walls protect us. We are all fully in the world, and the complexity of the world has grown exponentially. Instead, we are cut off from the world in other ways, like solitary hermits who wander the world carrying our caves on our backs. Although embedded in the world of action, we also can feel the depths of loneliness while surrounded by many others. To surmount these barriers, we are called to be both deeply reflective and active outwardly. As Dag Hammarskjöld wrote, "In our era, the road to holiness necessarily passes through the world of action."[7] If this feels contradictory, it is. A new paradoxical geometry of life has gradually established itself at the core of modern existence. It is right and proper that we lead our active lives, fully engaged in the world, but amid the rush of the outer world, we must keep in mind the words of the Trappist monk Thomas Merton: "To allow oneself to be carried away by a multitude of conflicting concerns, to surrender to too many demands, to commit to too many projects, to want to help everyone in everything is itself to succumb to

---

7. Dag Hammarskjöld, *Markings*, trans. W. H. Auden, Leif Sjoberg (NY: Vintage Books, 2006).

the violence of our times."[8] We need to complement our outer work with a comparable commitment to inner work, but for most this will occur without retreating to monastic communities. We therefore require a form of practice that reflects the changed times in which we live, and the particular form of consciousness we carry.

The method of *contemplative inquiry* that I will unfold in this book attempts to answer this call by incorporating the contemplative life into the active life. Good intentions and technical skills, essential though they are, will not be sufficient to make us into the educators, doctors, statesmen, scientists, and artists needed in the future. In this I agree with the assessment of the ecologist John Milton, who maintains that political, legal, and economic approaches to progress simply do not go deep enough. "By themselves they won't bring about the penetrating changes in human culture that we need for people to live in true harmony and balance with one another and the earth. The next great opening of an ecological worldview will have to be an internal one."[9]

This opening to the internal can build on the sound foundations of methods such as mindfulness-based stress reduction (MBSR), which have proved skillful vehicles for universalizing the profoundly transformative and healing practices, insights, and realizations at the heart of the meditative tradition. Such systematic meditative practice and inquiry have now entered and benefited a wide range of mainstream institutions and fields, including medicine and health care, business, the law, and education, by introducing deep insights that reach beyond the reductionist, materialist conception of our world and "reality" that is so prevalent today. That some eminent scientists assert that all of nature and humanity are purely material does not make it true. Such metaphysical suppositions have nothing to do with the success of their scientific theories. We require new and more embracing methods of inquiry that can accommodate the great advances of science but not be limited by the dogmatic perspective of materialism and its associated economics. These views of humanity and

---

8. Thomas Merton, *Conjectures of a Guilty Bystander* (NY: Doubleday, 1968).
9. Quoted in Peter Senge, C. Otto Scharmer, Joseph Jaworski and Betty Sue Flowers, *Presence*, (Cambridge, MA: SoL, 2004), p. 66.

our cosmos are simply too narrow and impoverished to succeed. I agree with those who have maintained that the true goal of contemplative practice, indeed of life, is the joining of insight and compassion, wisdom and love. In creating the internal opening Milton advocates, contemplative inquiry can, I believe, cultivate these qualities and give rise to the kinds of insights that are needed in all domains of life.

The relation between knowledge and contemplative striving has a long history. Buddhism views the root source of suffering as ignorance concerning the true nature of the world and ourselves. Insight or *vipassana* is, therefore, considered essential to enlightenment or liberation. On a personal level, each of us carries concerns begging for clarity. They may be prompted by the illness of a child, a social crisis, or our deep concern for the environment. We are occupied with issues at home, at work, and in our community. How can we cultivate genuine insight and so find better ways of addressing them? In my life as an educator, scientist, activist, father, and writer, I have come to rely on contemplative inquiry as a trusted means of moving beyond brooding and intellectual analysis to what I experience as insights that bear with them the feel of truth, and which also have proven fruitful in life. Most of the good I have done has its roots in contemplative reflection of this kind.

As a scientist who delights in the clarity of physics and in the profound philosophical puzzles it poses, I do not seek a diminishment of science but rather a transformation and extension of its methods. The same values of clarity, integrity and collegiality can infuse contemplative exploration as have supported natural scientific exploration. Once we appreciate the full multidimensional nature of the human being and of our universe, we will be better equipped to deal with its problems.

Through both science and meditation I have sought insight into our world and the means to be of service. What follows is a guide to contemplative practice and inquiry for those who, like me, have a longing to know and, at the same time, to be of help. I have found Rudolf Steiner's work to be a prime example of contemplation as a path of knowledge, and one that has led to many applications in education, agriculture and medicine. My personal meditative practice has been guided by his advice at every step, and much of what I present here is based on his writings and on my attempt over many years to practice according to his recommendations.

The following pages contain a selection of the contemplative exercises that I have personally found useful, many of which I have come to include in my teaching at Amherst College. The students I have taught have told me how helpful these exercises have been to them personally as well as in deepening their engagement with the material we have covered. Encouraged by my experience with them, as well as in my own life, I would like to share with you my view of meditation and what it offers us.

I have organized this book in a way that first gives the reader an overview of the contemplative path, as I see it. Following this overview I return to the beginning and offer more detailed instruction for the full range of practices familiar to me. The later chapters will journey far into the work of contemplative inquiry. They will ask much of the reader, but the gains for ourselves and our world are large and, in my opinion, essential to the "great opening" that will be necessary for our future.

In writing this book I have continually struggled to find a language that is at once accessible and authentic. Much of the language of meditation has been co-opted, commercialized, or otherwise distorted, and religious or spiritual terminology has also become an obstacle for many. As a consequence, while I may use spiritual language where it seems necessary, I attempt to stay close to the practices themselves and the experiences that arise through them. Readers who would like to situate these practices and experiences within the religious and spiritual literature will be pointed to the relevant resources.

I present these exercises and commentary as a simple practitioner, not as a guru in a particular sect. While we can certainly admire those who demonstrate great learning and compassion, the time for unquestioning devotion and obedience to a teacher is past. The reader, therefore, should treat all that is said here as the suggestions of someone who has practiced meditation as a complement to the scientific and practical life. What has proven helpful to me may not be helpful to others; each reader will have to test the methods and practices I present to determine what is appropriate. In this sense, while we receive advice, we are our own teachers. We are each able to assess the extent to which practices are supportive of our lives. While I take responsibility for writing down the words within these pages, you the reader must take responsibility as well. I hope you will find the journey rewarding.

Chapter One

Overview of the Path

The longest journey is the journey inward.

— Dag Hammarskjöld

Before taking up specific exercises, we need to consider the nature of solitude and its place in contemplative practice. In addition we will concern ourselves with the ethical foundation of meditation, which is essential for a proper orientation to the contemplative path. With these preliminaries behind us we can then turn to the varieties of practice, first those that are intended to buttress our psychological health and secondly those that draw our inner gaze beyond the self. We will move from the establishment of humility and reverence as fundamental moods to the cultivation of inner harmony, emotional balance, and attention. With these inner accomplishments we can take up the selfless work of meditation and contemplative inquiry whose fruits can be of use to ourselves and others.

This chapter will provide a short overview of the path as I understand it. Consider it as an overture to the fuller treatment given in subsequent chapters. The elements, themes, and motifs announced here will be expanded and explored amply later. I will give a deeper treatment of the stages and difficulties associated with the contemplative journey, together with many suggestions for exercises. As we set out we should remember that although the horizon of contemplative practice is infinite, each and every step we take is already of inestimable value.

Contemporary Contemplative Inquiry

On August 12, 1904, Rainer Maria Rilke wrote to the young poet Franz Kappus concerning solitude:

> To speak of solitude again, it becomes always clearer that this is at bottom not something that one can take or leave. We *are* solitary. We may delude ourselves and act as though this were not so. That is all. But how much better it is to realize that we are so, yes, even to set out by assuming it.[10]

Contemplative practice means, among other things, becoming practiced in solitude. This does not mean brooding or self-indulgent musing, but instead practicing a special form of recollection of the past, mindfulness for the present, and envisioning of the future in a manner that is enlivening, clear, and insightful. We learn to be properly solitary, and to carry the depth of our solitude into the world with grace and selflessness.

Therefore it is important to set aside times for reflection, contemplative exercises, and meditation. It may be thirty minutes in the morning or evening or both. Regardless of the amount of time spent, the fruits of such activity are many and significant. For example, when we practice finding a right relationship to the troublesome thoughts and feelings that occupy our inner life, we learn to form right judgments and habits of mind that benefit us in daily life. The angry reaction that would normally leap from our lips or the violence we might let loose on our momentary adversary is caught short. We have come to know the troubling dynamic well from having rehearsed it inwardly, and now the real-world version no longer finds us off guard and unaware. We grow to become, as Daniel Goleman terms it, "emotionally intelligent."[11] I will return to this and other benefits of contemplative practice later, but my point here is that long after the practice session is over, its fruits continue to appear.

---

10. Rilke letter of August 12, 1904, to Franz Kappus, trans. Stephen Mitchell, *Letters to a Young Poet* (New York: Vintage, 1986), p. 87; or the German in *Von Kunst und Leben*, p. 159.
11. Daniel Goleman, *Emotional Intelligence* (New York: Bantam Books, 1995).

We need not, in fact should not, attempt to meditate all the time. The time we set aside for it in the morning or evening should have a start and a finish. The fruits of meditation, however, will penetrate all aspects of our life, benefiting not only us but others as well. Setting aside times specifically for contemplative practice may be the most obvious and yet sometimes the most difficult part of the work. It inevitably seems that once the time and place to sit has been found, a forgotten cell phone rings, or the cry of a beloved child pierces the early morning air and closed door. In such moments we sense the truth of the saying that the descent into the stillness of meditation seems to evoke turmoil.

If we are able to move beyond such distractions, whether they are external or internal, the time we give to a practice session can change everything. This time is important, and our appreciation of that importance can help us to make space for it in our busy lives. Certainly contemplative practice can invigorate us and help to settle the turmoil of life, but it also offers the occasion for something more. Through meditation I turn to aspects of the world and myself that I otherwise tend to neglect (such as wandering attention, uncalled-for irritability, and the like), and I do so with a quality of attention that is rare in normal life. We often forget the grandeur of the world we inhabit as well as the mystery of our lives. The simple act of stopping to reflect, and then of holding our awareness— gently but firmly—on these forgotten dimensions of the world and our lives is a service and even a duty. Do you not pause to attend to the child you love even though you are busy? Can you not likewise pause to cultivate solitude, which is the true place of beginning?

Once recognized, silence can become as important as sound, inaction as essential to us as action. Each partner in the pair balances and grounds the other. Once we have discovered this sacral dimension of our contemplative work, its significance increases and we turn to it more readily. I come to realize that in the end this work is not about me, my improvement or development. Contemplation is far more objective and its value far more real than I first recognized. My inner activity while meditating has intrinsic worth. Getting started is important not merely for me, but for its own sake.

Contemplative practice within a group, especially with guidance from a trusted and competent teacher, is often experienced as easier. The presence of others and the efforts they are making seem to resonate with our own effort, enhancing and compensating for the meagerness of our resources. Yet the work of meditation is, in the end, a solitary work. It is ours to do, and no amount of assistance can or should relieve us of it. Collective meditation should be guided by the principle of freedom within the group. As long as our individuality is honored, or, in Rilke's language, as long as our solitude is respected and protected, then our work in freedom with others can be an in important aid.

Solitude is more than a key to contemplative practice. As Rudolf Steiner once stated and Rilke emphasized, solitude is in fact the main characteristic of our modern age, and will become ever more so in the future.[12] Rilke identified the origins of this characteristic with the birth of modern lyric poetry. In his essay "Modern Lyric" of 1898, the twenty-three-year-old Rilke pointed to 1292 as the dawn of the modern lyric, the birth of poetry and literature as we know it. The event to which Rilke refers is the publication by Dante of his small collection of poems entitled *Vita nuova* (*The New Life*) in which a description of his unrequited love for Beatrice was given to the world. For Rilke, Dante's poems and his solitary struggle with love marked the onset of the central characteristic of modern human consciousness: solitude. "Since the first attempt of the individual to *find himself* in the flood of fleeting events, since the first struggle in the midst of the clamor of daily life to hearken to the deepest solitude of one's own being—there has been the modern lyric" (Rilke's emphasis).[13]

Hence "in the midst of the clamor of daily life" we are already hermits and will remain so for a long time to come. As a modern soul one is called to the "deepest solitude of one's own being." Our task is therefore not to deny this fact but to accept it and move forward with that certain understanding. Through patient practice we can deepen the quiet we all carry in us. Surprisingly, we will discover through solitude that a new fullness to human relationships unfolds, and we will learn to practice a new kind of love that can flourish between solitudes. Instead of isolating us, solitude

---

12. Rudolf Steiner, *Die Verbindung zwishen Lebenden und Toten*, Gesamtausgabe 168 (Dornach, Switz.: Rudolf Steiner Verlag, 1995), pp. 94–95.
13. Rainer Maria Rilke, "Moderne Lyrik" in *Von Kunst und Leben* (Frankfurt am Main: Insel Verlag, 2001), p. 9 (my translation).

will connect us to the depth of the other in ways that were impossible before.[14] The love that treasures the individual—the solitude of the other—is the principle on which we will one day build communities based on freedom.[15] Going forward, solitude and love will be inseparable.

The Cultivation of Virtue

When the meditative schooling of attention first made its way into the West from Asia, one of the first groups to take advantage of it was the Mossad, Israel's version of the CIA. The usefulness of *samadhi* or "single-pointed attention" to them was obvious. The ends to which they were directing their attention were classified. Since then many military organizations, basketball teams, and businesses have used contemplative methods to enhance their performance and reduce stress. I raise this issue less because I want to debate the appropriateness of teaching meditation to commandos (the martial arts have long combined meditation with martial action) than because I wish to point out the disconnection between virtue and contemplative practice. Meditation, even meditative accomplishment, does not automatically guarantee that the meditant will possess good moral judgment or practice an ethical life.

Stories to this effect are legion, both ancient and modern. The Indian sage Milarepa (c. 1052–1135) is said to have used his miraculous *siddhis* or psychic powers to bring devastation to an avaricious landlord who treated his parents inhumanely. Anger management problems have evidently been an issue for a long time even among masters. In recent years it seems that nearly every spiritual tradition has been plagued by financial or sexual scandals. Skilled and well-intentioned teachers are not immune to these temptations. All this points to a fundamental truth, namely, for meditative practice to have value as a positive contribution to the world it must rest on the foundations of a separate effort committed to moral development. In the Buddhist tradition this is called *sila* or "virtue," and it is held to be

---

14. Thomas Merton, "Love and Solitude," *Love and Living*, ed. Naomi Burton and Brother Patrick Hart (New York: Harcourt Brace, 1985).
15. Arthur Zajonc, "Dawning of Free Communities for Collective Wisdom," http://www.collectivewisdominitiative.org/papers/zajonc_dawning.htm.

the cornerstone of the Noble Eightfold Path. Within this tradition the practices of right speech, right action, and right livelihood are understood as essential to moral development. For those undertaking training within the Buddhist tradition, ethical precepts or rules are observed: five for lay practitioners and 227 rules for a fully ordained monk.

In our own time the strict adherence to a set of precepts, no matter how carefully formulated and well-intended, rightly violates our sense of autonomy. We may value moral guidance, but we ourselves have become the final arbiters of moral judgment. We possess the ability, if we quiet our passions, to discern clearly the right choice in any situation. When the medieval mystic Marguerite Porete wrote of the virtues, "I take leave of you." she was burned at the stake for the "Heresy of the Free Spirit."[16] She was ahead of her time in asserting that her love of God would be sufficient to guide her life. Linking her views to her renowned predecessor, she quoted St. Augustine's famous line, "Love, love, and do what you will," but that did not help. The Church could only envisage the chaos that would ensue if everyone followed his or her own sense of right and wrong. While we can sympathize with them, it now seems clear that the moral conditions for contemplative practice cannot and need not be imposed from the outside. In a sense, we are all (or should be) heretics of the free spirit.

Instead of rules, the practitioner can cultivate a set of moods or fundamental attitudes that are conducive to virtue. When practice is grounded in these moods or attitudes one feels that a proper moral foundation has been laid. The first mood is that of *humility*. Steiner calls humility the portal or gate through which the contemplative must pass.[17] Through it we set self-interest aside and acknowledge the high value of the other. Humility leads out onto the "path of *reverence*." Here I am not speaking of reverence for a person, but rather of reverence for the high principles that we seek to embody. The fundamental moods of humility and reverence are incompatible with egotism, which is a source of much moral confusion.

---

16. Marguerite Porete, *The Mirror of the Simple Soul in Medieval Writings on Female Spirituality*, ed. Elizabeth Spearing (New York: Penguin, 2002), p. 120ff.
17. Rudolf Steiner, *How to Know Higher Worlds* (Hudson, NY: Anthroposophic Press, 1994), p. 17.

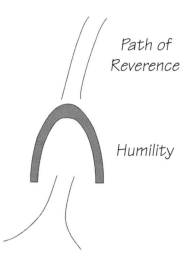

How do we cultivate these attitudes at the outset of a practice session? Here, as always, the individual must be taken into account. What will work for one will hinder another. For the medieval mystics, prayer was a sure doorway; these meditants, like many today, used the words of scripture to cultivate humility and devotion. Other modern contemplatives, however, may find their association with traditional religion to be so problematic that prayer is simply impossible. Many find the way to humility and reverence more easily via the wonder and awe inspired by nature's splendor. Calling to mind the starry night sky or the blue vault of heaven, or perhaps a favorite retreat of our own, such as a special rock, tree, or riverbank, can help us find our way to the portal of humility and the path of reverence.

In many individuals with whom I have worked, I have sensed the deep peace and simple joy they experience on finding the place of inner devotion when they spend time in the practice of prayer or meditation on nature. They often wish to linger here and deepen their devotion, cultivating it not just as a step on the path to contemplative inquiry but as a practice in its own right. While I will speak to this possibility later, for our purposes now we will acknowledge the power of humility, reverence, and devotion, and recognize that these attitudes provide a sound moral foundation for meditation. Their cultivation is a practice in virtue. Every contemplative practice session should begin by passing through the portal of humility and finding the path of reverence.

Inner Well-Being

When first we withdraw from outer activity and attend to the mind we are amazed at the rollicking confusion that generally prevails. Thoughts career in, as though from nowhere. Our mental day-planner suddenly shows up with three pressing and forgotten engagements that simply must be noted down before we forget them. Or our mind turns to a recent argument with our spouse, and what we should have said to make our case... and so on. At first the very idea that the mind can be still, lucid, and under my control seems a remote likelihood if not an impossibility. Emotions long forgotten or suppressed re-emerge; thoughts seem to possess an irrepressible life, spawning new ones via an associative logic all their own. With the mind in this state, little can be expected of meditation. Therefore the initial task is the cultivation of a mental and emotional balance or inner well-being. Think of it as inner hygiene, if you like. It is an essential and recurrent part of practice, one we never leave behind.

Taxonomies of mental afflictions and negative emotions can be found in Western as well as in Buddhist psychology. Indeed, Buddhism speaks of eighty-four thousand kinds of negative emotion! Yet all eighty-four thousand boil down to five core problems: hatred, desire, confusion, pride, and jealousy.[18] Another useful way to organize disturbances is based on a threefold picture of the inner life of the human being: thinking, feeling, and willing. Each of these areas can show pathological tendencies, which can be noticed by the meditant and for which contemplative exercises can be given. The first order of business, therefore, concerns practices designed to mitigate such disturbances. While there are many such exercises, several of which I will give in chapter three, the exercise I give here is based on one suggested by Rudolf Steiner and concerns care for our emotional life.[19]

Normally, we view experiences, emotions, and thoughts from inside. We identify with them. They are us, we are them. In this sense we are

---

18. Daniel Goleman, *Destructive Emotions* (New York: Bantam Books, 2003), p. 78; B. Alan Wallace, *Tibetan Buddhism from the Ground Up* (Boston: Wisdom Publication, 1993), Chapter 5.
19. Steiner, *How to Know Higher Worlds*, pp. 26–31.

enmeshed in our emotions and thoughts, and we experience a sense of self or identity through them. Such an experience of self is a delusion and a source of problems. The first exercise, therefore, has been selected to provide us with some distance from our own experiences, allowing us to consider them from the outside and work with them from a new vantage point. The discovery of that new and higher vantage point is not always easy, but once we learn the way to it, then the narrow pathway to emotional equanimity can open and allow us to consider the most intense emotional struggles of daily life gracefully from the viewpoint familiar to us from meditation. By way of introduction, I relate an episode from the life of the American civil rights leader Dr. Martin Luther King Jr.

During his years of work on behalf of black Americans, Martin Luther King ceaselessly advocated for nonviolent action as a means of drawing attention to the oppression of blacks, especially in the South. He received many threats and suffered several attempts on his life. In one instance his home in Montgomery, Alabama, was bombed while he was at a church meeting.[20] The porch and front of the house were heavily damaged. His wife, Coretta, and daughter Yoki were in the back of the house at the time, and no one was hurt. By the time the King arrived, an agitated crowd of hundreds of black neighbors had gathered, ready to retaliate against the police who were there. Their much-loved leader and his family had been attacked. Facing the strong possibility of a race riot, the police asked King if he would address the crowd. King went out onto what remained of his front porch, held up his hands and everyone grew quiet. He said,

> We believe in law and order. Don't do anything panicky at all. Don't get your weapons. He who lives by the sword will perish by the sword. Remember that is what God said. We are not advocating violence. We want to love our enemies. I want you to love our enemies. Be good to them. Love them and let them know you love them. I did not start this boycott. I was asked by you to serve as your spokesman. I want it known the length and breadth of this land that if I am stopped this movement will not stop. If I am stopped our work will not stop.

---

20. Martin Luther King, Jr., *The Autobiography of Martin Luther King*, Jr., ed. Clayborne Carson (New York: IPM/ Warner Books, 2001), Chapter 8.

For what we are doing is right. What we are doing is just. And God is with us.

When Martin finished, everyone went home without violence, saying "Amen" and "God bless you." Tears were on many faces. Surely King had felt the same emotions of anger at the attempt on the lives of his family and himself, but he was also able to find a place in himself from which he could speak and act that did not answer hate with hate, but instead could meet hate with love.

In our own lives we experience similar if smaller affronts, but they can lead to long periods of brooding anger and internal agitation. The contemplative exercise begins by selecting from out of past experience an occasion of hatred, jealousy, desire, anger, etc. It should be strong but not overwhelming or too recent. Then, after having found your way to the gateway of humility and the path of reverence, relive the occasion selected. As you call the situation back to mind, it is important to allow the associated negative emotions (desire, pride, anger…) to rise up once again. Feel their force, sense the stir of feelings and the undertow that, if left unchecked, might well lead you back into the dark, uncontrolled emotions of the original situation. Only by allowing these feelings some sway can we practice overcoming them and so learn to hold the situation in a new light. As the emotions begin to take hold, like the arrival of Martin Luther King's angry neighbors, look within yourself for higher ground, for a place from which to inwardly behold yourself and the entire situation. Encompass the conflicting parts of the drama with your field of attention. Feel the contention between two selves. Move away from the undertow of destructive emotions and take up your place as a witness. Find your way from the mentality of the crowd to the Martin Luther King in you. From your new vantage point, go on to experience the inner dynamics that are at play in the situation.

To come under the sway of negative emotions is to be blinded. When carried away by anger, lust, or jealousy we do not really see who or what is before us. We cannot judge the forces at play or intuit the right way forward. Now, from the new vantage point, attempt to see who really stands before you and what forces are actually active. In the midst of the occurrence, sense the history behind it and the possibility that lies beyond it. The events of the day and indeed your entire life have led to the encounter and to the negative emotions. They are factors that can be seen and appreciated.

If others are involved, imagine them in like manner. They too bring a history and future to the encounter; they too lived through events unknown to you during that day. Do not psychoanalyze yourself or the other person. Rather, simply appreciate, sympathetically and objectively, the complexity and multiple dimensions of the drama that is unfolding. It is not a question of right or wrong but of compassionate understanding. The emotional force of the exchange, though still present, is now viewed and held differently. When we speak and act from this place of compassionate understanding, we are better able to disperse the angry mob, and to answer hate with love.

If we are sailing on the high seas and a storm hits, how do we respond? To simply curse the wind and crashing waves would be immature as well as ineffective. Far better to accept the fact of the storm, over which we have no control, and turn our attention to that over which we do have control, namely ourselves and the sailboat. How much sail should we have up, what should be the heading, is the cargo tied down and are the hatches shut? Life presents us with storms and trials. Often they are not of our making, but how we handle them is. This exercise is, therefore, not designed to empty us of emotion but rather to help guide us through high seas.

It should be clear that we cultivate equanimity *not* so as to be better prepared for a counter attack, but rather so we can find an opening for understanding and reconciliation. From the vantage point of the helm or the high ground we may well discover the petty basis for our jealousies or the illusory grounds for our desires. The insight so gained does not automatically lead to the destruction of jealousy and desire. It is much harder to live our insights than to have them! Nevertheless, a beginning is made by not giving ourselves over to our emotions, but pausing to set aside egotism, seek higher ground, discover the Martin Luther King in ourselves, and so hold the conflict in a far more generous pair of hands. I sometimes call this the Martin Luther King exercise because King, while still possessed of human frailties, seemed so often to live, speak, and act from a high place beyond ego that we can call the "the silent self."

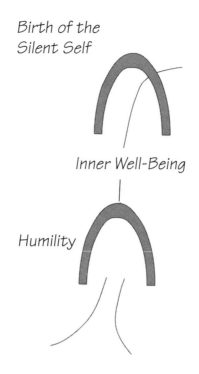

Birth of the Silent Self

Inner Well-Being

Humility

Birth of the Silent Self

In an essay for a student newspaper Thomas Merton wrote of the importance of creative silence in which one turns from what he called the "social self," which is defined by our manifold interactions with others, toward a "deeper, silent self"[21]—the calm captain of the sailboat or the witness on the hillside. King had found his way innumerable times to this deeper, silent self and so could speak and act from it rather than succumbing to the mob mentality. To reawaken ourselves as Thoreau exhorts us to do, we need to give birth to the silent self in the midst of our conventional life of duty and desire. The cultivation of deep, inner well-being can culminate in the birth of the silent self that is usually obscured and forgotten.

The poet Juan Ramón Jiménez captures the mystery of our deepest identity—our silent self—in his poem "I am not I."

---

21. Thomas Merton, reprinted in the *Bulletin of Monastic Interreligious Dialogue*, no. 67, August 2001, p. 1. Also online at www.monasticdialog.com/bulletins/67/merton.htm.

I am not I.
I am this one
Walking beside me whom I do not see,
Whom at times I manage to visit,
And whom at other times I forget;
The one who remains silent when I talk,
The one who forgives, sweet, when I hate,
The one who takes a walk where I am not,
The one who will remain standing when I die.[22]

Jiménez touches here on the great mystery of our true identity. We will not unravel it in a few lines, but the experience is unmistakable. Having passed through the portal of humility and found the path of reverence, the gradual calming of the mind, together with the enhancement of attention, silences the social self. In the contemplative space that then opens out in us, the common ego vanishes and we begin to operate with what Jiménez calls the not-I. Typically unnoticed, only it endures, only it will remain standing when I die. That is to say, all outer aspects of my persona (gender, profession, factual knowledge…) will pass away, and only the not-I will endure. In Buddhism this is the turn toward *an-atman* or No-Self; in Christianity it is the discovery of the "not I but Christ in me" of St. Paul. It is as if we shift our mode of awareness from center to periphery and in doing so we experience everything anew.[23] An act that was met with anger, or an encounter that stimulated desire, shifts with the birth of the not-I. The anger may well be justified, and we can even value the feeling of moral outrage before turning toward the not-I. Yet once we do birth the not-I we meet our anger or sorrows differently, as King met the angry crowd.

Rumi began his life not as a poet and mystic but as a scholar of Islamic literature and philosophy. His meeting with the mystic Shams-i-Tabriz at thirty-seven began the profound transformation, but it took the tragic

---

22. In *The Winged Energy of Delight*, trans. Robert Bly (NY: Harper Perennial, 2005).

23. Language fails us in attempting to describe the not-I. As in negative theology or the *via negativa*, the dangers associated with describing the positive attributes of a higher self are unavoidable.

loss of Shams three years later, and the uncontrollable grief that followed, to open up the floodgates of poetry, song, and spiritual communion. It took Rumi many months to turn from the self that only saw loss to the no-self or silent self that could rediscover an inner relationship to Shams even after his passing. When we read Rumi's poem "The Guest House" we do well to remember the depth of his sufferings and sorrows.[24]

> This being human is a guest house.
> Every morning a new arrival.
>
> A joy, a depression, a meanness,
> some momentary awareness comes
> as an unexpected visitor.
>
> Welcome and entertain them all!
> Even if they're a crowd of sorrows,
> who violently sweep your house
> empty of its furniture, still,
> treat each guest honorably.
> He may be clearing you out
> for some new delight.
>
> The dark thought, the shame, the malice,
> meet them at the door laughing
> and invite them in.
>
> Be grateful for whoever comes
> because each has been sent
> as a guide from beyond.

All that we have of Rumi, his poetry and dervish dancing, arose with the birth of his silent self, or with the birth of a higher I that has nothing

---

24. *Rumi: The Book of Love*, trans. Coleman Barks (New York: HarperCollins, 2003), p. 179.

in common with the conventional social self. The loss of his beloved Shams: even this, Rumi learned to welcome and treat honorably. Surely, his meeting with Shams—his true spiritual friend—was "sent as a guide from beyond," but so too was his loss. From that loss streamed the thousands of lines that comprise his great poetic work the Mathnawi, known for centuries as "the Qur'an in Pahlavi."

In my experience, if we have practiced the Martin Luther King exercise in the quiet of contemplation, then when we encounter a comparable situation in real life a new resource is available to us. We still meet our nemesis or have that dreaded, fearful confrontation, but now as our emotions rise and the undertow starts to pull, we turn automatically in search of higher ground. We seek out and find the narrow path that leads us to the silent self, a path we often missed in the past. When the onslaught hits we walk a path we have cleared from destructive emotions to generosity. As a consequence, our words and actions originate from a different source, one that seeks mutual understanding and reconciliation instead of victory. We may also find that this way of being in the moment calls forth a like response in the person opposite us. The people we encounter may find themselves speaking with uncommon generosity. It sometimes happens that, in place of violence, respect for one another may emerge, and with it a new beginning to a relationship.

This practice speaks to only one problematic aspect of the inner life, but it can be of enormous help if taken up and practiced consistently. I will describe other practices for inner well-being in chapter three. Through them we ultimately seek not merely to control our emotions but to so transform ourselves that we are generous and gracious by nature in life. Instead of managing our emotions, we are to become different people, in whom these positive characteristics are intrinsic. Such changes do not occur quickly. We are a medium that is remarkably resistant to change. If I use the metaphor of a sculpture, then we are at one and the same time the stubborn stone, the transforming chisel, and the artist's guiding hands. The physicist Erwin Schrödinger wrote:[25]

---

25. Erwin Schrödinger, *What Is Life? Mind and Matter* (London: Cambridge University Press, 1967), p. 107.

And thus at every step, on every day of our life, as it were, something of the shape that we possessed until then has to change, to be overcome, to be deleted and replaced by something new. The resistance of our primitive will is the psychical correlate of the resistance of the existing shape to the transforming chisel. For we ourselves are chisel and statue, conquerors and conquered at the same time—it is a true continued "self-conquering" (Selbstüberwindung).

If we come even part of the way toward the goal of self-transformation, then the world about us changes as well. It is seen with delight and a steady, open heart. We feel nourished as if by a hidden stream; we have patience and display good judgment. The first Psalm must have been written with this in mind.[26]

Blessed are the man and the woman
    who have grown beyond their greed
    and have put an end to their hatred
    and no longer nourish illusions.
But they delight in the way things are
    and keep their hearts open, day and night.
They are like trees planted near flowing rivers,
    which bear fruit when they are ready.
Their leaves will not fall or wither.
    Everything they do will succeed.

Meditation and Contemplative Inquiry

The Martin Luther King exercise was concerned with the establishment of a stable and healthy inner life, and with the birth of the silent self or not-I. If this foundation is absent then all further work will be in vain, leading only to delusions and projections. For this reason, preparation is essential to all subsequent contemplative practice. Yet contemplative practice is not exclusively or even primarily concerned with our problems,

---

26. Stephen Mitchell, *The Enlightened Heart* (New York: Harper & Row, 1989), p. 5.

inattention, and afflictions, as important as these may be to us personally. At the center of practice is meditation proper, which is ultimately concerned with what is of value to all human beings. Perhaps better said, it is concerned with the true nature of things.

We understand that the laws of Euclidean geometry do not depend on me or my preferences. Likewise, the discoveries of science are true in all countries and in all times, otherwise antiretroviral drugs and cell phones would not work in Africa as well as America. The world is not organized around me, but has its own nature. When we go beyond exercises designed to promote inner hygiene, we meditate on the way things are. We seek what transcends our personal problems. This does not imply that we are disinterested in the human condition, only that the particular issues we struggle with are left behind. We seek through meditation to confront the depths and heights, the moral and spiritual realities that underlie all things.

I view this as a progression. Having entered through the portal of humility, found the path of reverence, cultivated an inner hygiene, and birthed the silent self, we undertake meditation proper. In meditation we move through a sequence of practices that starts with simple contemplative engagement and then deepen that engagement to sustained contemplative inquiry, which with grace can lead to contemplative insight or knowing.

Although it seeks for objectivity like conventional science, contemplative inquiry differs from science in a very important respect. Where conventional science strives to disengage or distance itself from direct experience for the sake of objectivity, contemplative inquiry does exactly the opposite. It seeks to engage direct experience, to participate more and more fully in the phenomena of consciousness. It achieves "objectivity" in a different manner, namely through self-knowledge and what Goethe in his scientific writings termed a "delicate empiricism."[27]

After working hygienically on one's mental distractions and emotional instability, the practitioner turns his or her attention away from the self and toward a set of thoughts and experiences that reaches far beyond one's

---

27. For more on Goethe's science see David Seamon and Arthur Zajonc, *Goethe's Way of Science* (Albany, NY: SUNY Press, 1998), or Henri Bortoft, *The Wholeness of Nature* (Hudson, NY: Lindisfarne Press, 1996).

personal life. The possible forms and contents for meditation at this stage are infinitely varied. Meditations can be word-based, image-based, sense-based, and so on. Each of these has something special to offer us, and each will be described in chapter four. Selecting a single flower from this rich bouquet, we can turn to the great spiritual literature of all times, or to the poets and sages who have given expression to thoughts and experiences that are of universal value. We find in them ample resources for meditation. For instance a passage from the Bible or the *Bhagavad Gita*, or a line from a poem by Emily Dickinson, can be used as the subject for meditation.

Take as an example the words attributed to Thales and which were said to have been inscribed on the wall of the Temple at Delphi: "Human being, know yourself!" At first this command seems to plunge us back into ourselves, but this need not be the case. We can take up these words in a way that addresses the human condition generally and not us partic-ularly. At the outset of the meditation, we can simply speak the words, repeating them again and again. Then we can move deeper to "live the words," holding each one at the center of our attention. With each word or phrase there is an associated image or concept. We work our way back and forth repeatedly between word, image, and concept. The words "know" and "yourself," for example, take on a multilayered, even infinite character. The meditative verse or line is like a star on the horizon, infi-nitely far away but providing orientation and inspiration.

Because of its richness there are innumerable ways of working with every meditation. For example, first I slowly sound the line several times inwardly, speaking it silently to myself. I give each word my full attention, sensing the meaning of each word. Once I have settled my attention onto these words, "Human being, know yourself!" I then shift the speaking voice so the words are sounded from out of the periphery, as if they were coming out of the wide reaches of space or from the hills and sky and earth. The words are spoken to me; they are a call from the larger landscape surrounding me. The call is specifically to me as a human being. It is a call to self-knowledge. I hear the call, I pause, and I take up the injunction.

I turn first to myself as physical human being. I sense the earthly, substantial aspect of myself: my physical body. I begin with my limbs, my hands and arms, my feet and legs. I may even move them slightly to feel their physical presence more fully. I then attend to my midsection, my chest and back. I feel my breath and the beating of my heart. These too are part of my physical nature. Finally I attend to my head, which rests quietly atop the body; its solid round form harbors the senses, now closed to the world. Limbs, midsection, and head form the physical human being. I picture each and their relation to one another. I know the physical human being. I rest for a time with this image and experience within me.

Next I turn to the inner life of thoughts, feelings, and intentions. I notice how my will is carried out mysteriously. My intentions to think or to act culminate, via ways that are unknown to me, in a coordinated flow of movement. I live in that activity, which I can direct. It is part of my nature. In addition I have a rich life of feelings. Feelings of sympathy or antipathy, of exhaustion or alertness, of excitement or remorse are present within me. I sense their importance for me, how much of my life is determined by them or reflected in them. Normally I am only partially conscious of their significance and only partly control them. Their domain is partly veiled yet open to my interest and responsive to my activity. No less than my physical body, these feelings constitute a part of my nature. Finally I turn to my thinking. My life of thought is at once my life and a participant in something that transcends me. I can communicate with others, share thoughts with them. This points to something universal in thinking: like all others, I participate in a universal stream of thinking activity. I know, through experiencing it inwardly, that thinking is a part of my nature.

All three—thinking, feeling, and willing—interweave to form a single self. I have intended every thought within my meditation (unless I have become distracted), and I feel the ebb and flow of feelings associated with each thought. Actions may well ensue from these. The three form a natural unity. They are like the limbs, the midsection, and the head: separable in thought but entwined in reality. All three are needed. All three are me. I quietly live into the three and the one.

Finally, I shift my attention away from the body and even away from my thoughts, feelings, and intentions. I attend instead to a presence or activity that animates but transcends all of these. It lights up in thinking but is not the thought content I experience. This third aspect of myself is the most elusive and invisible, and yet I sense it is the essential and universal aspect that is both truly me and not me alone. I only sense it in reflection. It might be considered my Self, but in a way that is not gendered or aged or possessed of any particular characteristics. Without it I would be body and mind, physical matter, feelings, thoughts, and habitual intentions, but my originality and genius would be missing. In the language of Thoreau's morning reflections, I would forever be condemned to sleep, because this agency alone has the possibility to waken me to a poetic and divine life. In turning my attention towards this silent self, I sense the intimations of a Self that is no-self. I recognize it also as a part of me, or perhaps I am a part of it.

I then hold together all three aspects—body, soul, and spirit—in the space of my meditation. All of them are me; each is real and present. I feel their presence, their reality, separately and together. I sustain this feeling for as long as I can, and then with clear intention, I empty my consciousness of these images and ideas. I empty myself completely, but I hold my attention open and live silently in the meditative space thus prepared. I have shaped the emptiness with my activity. Now that the space of my meditation is empty of my content, of my thoughts and feelings, I can sustain an open attention without expectation and without grasping. Not attempting to see or hear, I nonetheless may sense or experience something echoing back into that space, presencing itself for a shorter or longer time, changing and then disappearing. Waiting, not grasping, one is grateful. In the words of the *Tao Te Ching*,[28]

> Do you have the patience to wait
> till your mud settles and the water is clear?
> Can you remain unmoving
> till the right action arises by itself?
>
> The Master doesn't seek fulfillment.
> Not seeking, not expecting
> she is present, and can welcome all things.

I have learned to welcome all things. A deep peacefulness settles into the body and mind. I rest within that peace in gratitude. Sensing that the meditation is complete, I turn back.

---

28. Stephen Mitchell, *Tao Te Ching* (New York:HarperCollins, 1988), p. 15.

In meditation we move between focused and open attention. We give our full attention to the individual words of our chosen text, and to their associated images and meanings. Then we move to their relationship to each other so that a living organism of thought is experienced. We allow this experience to intensify by holding the complex of meanings inwardly before us. We may need to re-sound the words, to elaborate the images, to reconstruct the meanings, and to feel again their interrelationships in order to hold on to and intensify the experience. After a period of vivid concentration on the content of meditation, the content is released. That which was held is gone. Our attention opens. We are entirely present. An interior psychic space has been intently prepared, and we remain in that space. We wait, not expecting, not hoping, but present to welcome whatever may or may not arise within the infinite stillness. If a shy, dawning experience emerges into the space we have prepared, then we gratefully and gently greet it: not grasping, not seeking.

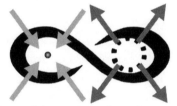

Focused Attention   Open Attention

I view this as a kind of "breathing" of attention. First we are intently focused on an object of contemplation, but then the object is released and our open, non-focal awareness is sustained. We are breathing not air but the inner light of the mind—what I call *cognitive breathing*. In it we live in a slow tempo, alternating between focused attention and openness. As we breathe the light of attention, we sense a shift in our state of consciousness during the meditation. Feelings of expansion and union, vitality and movement may follow. Such feelings may become especially apparent during the phase of open attention.

While walking across the Boston Common in a state of reflection Ralph Waldo Emerson described his inner experience in vivid terms: "...my head bathed by the blithe air and uplifted into infinite space—all mean egotism vanishes. I become a transparent eyeball; I am nothing; I see all; the currents of the Universal being circulate through me."[29] In this famous passage Emerson writes of participating in a reality larger than himself, one that reaches far beyond the small ego of conventional consciousness. His social self, his persona has vanished, and the currents of the Universal being circulate through him. Emerson's experience places before us the complex issue of contemplative experience.

The Journey Home

The journey home is as important as the journey out. Having lived our way out through the words, "Human being, know yourself," we can sound them once again inwardly as we return. When we first heard these four words their fullness was not yet apparent, but now that we have meditated them a depth or aura of meaning pervades them. On the return journey we hear the words differently; they carry within them layers of experience and images. We seek to integrate that richness of experience into our lives as we journey home.

We have been born to a life of service and tasks. These are important. Meditation is no escape. It is only a preparation for life. We come back to ourselves deepened, more awake, and reaffirmed by our contact with the infinite, with the mysteries of our own nature, with the divine. If our meditation has been successful, we may even be reluctant to return home. Such reluctance, however, is not in keeping with the moral foundations of love and selflessness we laid at the outset. The fruits of the meditative life are not for us to hoard but to share. Contemplation is properly undertaken as a selfless act of service, and so the return home is the true goal. If we have lived rightly into the sacred space of meditation then we will be more fit, more insightful, more loving in life.

If we entered through the portal of humility, then we exit through the portal of gratitude. There are an infinite number of ways to say thank you. So too are there countless ways to close a meditation session. In the

---

29. Ralph Waldo Emerson, "Nature 1836," *Selected Essays* edited by Larzer Ziff (New York: Penguin Books, 1992) p. 39.

Buddhist tradition one seals the meditation by dedicating its fruits to benefit all sentient beings that they may be free from suffering. In other traditions one closes with a prayer of gratitude, such as Psalm 131:[30]

> Lord, my mind is not noisy with desires,
>> and my heart has satisfied its longing.
> I do not care about religion
>> or anything that is not you.
> I have soothed and quieted my soul,
>> like a child at its mother's breast.
> My soul is as peaceful as a child
>> sleeping in its mother's arms.

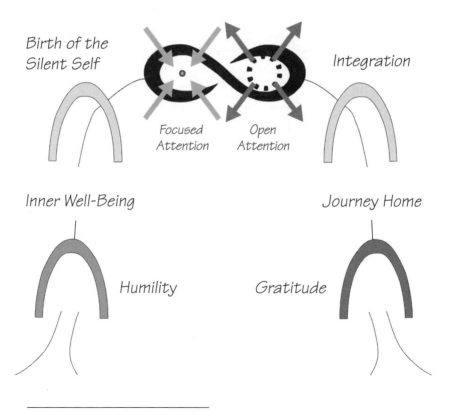

---

30. Psalm 131, trans. Stephen Mitchell, *The Enlightened Heart*.

Contemplative Experience

With contemplative practice comes contemplative experience, whether of the type reported by Emerson or myriad other variants. What are we to make of such experiences?

The contemplative traditions take a wide range of viewpoints concerning the significance of experiences had during meditation. What is the proper attitude of the contemplative toward such experience? At one extreme we find the sixteenth-century words of St. John of the Cross, himself a deep contemplative. After laying out with remarkable precision a list of contemplative experiences, he advises that we turn away from all such as distractions from the main task as he saw it, the establishment of faith.

> We must disencumber the intellect of these spiritual apprehensions by guiding and directing it past them into the spiritual night of faith. A person should not store up or treasure the forms of these visions impressed within him, neither should he have the desire of clinging to them. In doing so, he would impede himself by what dwells within him (those forms, images, and figures of persons), and he would not journey to God through the negation of all things.... The more one desires darkness and annihilation of himself regarding all visions, exteriorly or interiorly receivable, the greater will be the infusion of faith and consequently of love and hope, since these three theological virtues increase together.[31]

Likewise, in the Buddhist tradition the experiences had during meditation are considered a sideshow on the path to enlightenment. They can become a new domain to which we become just as attached as to the sense world. As such, meditative experience can be viewed as another source of suffering and a detour or distraction from the ultimate goal. St. John of the Cross had many profound experiences, but like the Buddhists he also preached detachment, warning against our "desire to cling to them." This grasping impedes us on our journey to God, as he puts it.

---

31. St. John of the Cross, *The Ascent of Mt. Carmel*, Chapter 23.

St. John of the Cross therefore advocates that we embrace the deep and dark night of faith.

On the other hand, the Gnostic and mystical traditions of all peoples have treasured meditation's illumination of consciousness and the insights that derive from contemplative experience. Texts concerned with such experiences can be found in every indigenous culture and in every faith tradition. The Harvard psychologist William James sought out those who had had robust mystical experiences, and he wrote of the importance of a science of such experience. Rudolf Steiner's detailed presentation of his own experiences is an extraordinary example of a modern, scientifically oriented, and philosophically trained contemplative who is writing and speaking directly out of his meditative experience. I place myself within this contemplative lineage and believe that much benefit can derive from continued work in it. The potential value of contemplative experience—not only for the meditant, but also for society—requires that we take meditative experiences seriously.

In order for contemplative inquiry to take its place among humanity's cherished ways of coming to true insight, many must take up its methods, apply them with care and consistency, and communicate their experiences to one another to reach consensus. The stages of contemplative inquiry include all those I have described from the moral foundation of humility and reverence, through inner hygiene, to meditation on a particular content. That content can be a research issue or question. I will describe much more fully in later chapters the scope and practices of contemplative inquiry as I view it, but in brief it is the application of attentional breathing to one's research. I believe that in informal and unconscious ways this is already part of the discovery process of creative individuals.

While St. John and the Buddhists are right to warn us concerning the dangers of attachment to exceptional states of consciousness or extraordinary experiences, we can cultivate a healthy, non-grasping orientation toward them. Our attitude, not the experiences themselves, is the potential problem. It is therefore of paramount importance to create a right relationship to contemplative experience, lest it become a distraction from the main goal. In particular, one should refrain from exploiting experiences or even from interpreting them prematurely.

The healthiest attitude is that of simple acceptance, treating such experiences as unexpected phenomena whose significance will be given in time but that need not be understood immediately. The experiences had during meditation may be novel and wonderful, and we can note them appreciatively, but we should refrain from speaking about them except with a trusted teacher, colleague, or friend. In more advanced stages of meditative practice meaning does join to experience, but usually not at the outset. By this I mean that practices beyond what I have described in this chapter can so deepen our engagement that clear insight arises as an integral part of our meditation. We are on a path of knowledge, but patience above all is called for, and the egoism we aimed to leave behind at the first portal to meditation should not be allowed to cloud our vision here. The specifics of these practices will be described toward the end of the book.

While the meditative life is different for each person, key elements are common to most. As I have stressed, we must establish the right moral foundation for meditation through cultivating the attitudes of humility, reverence and selflessness. The true foundation for meditative life is that of love. Once we walk through the portal of humility we soon discover the turmoil of our inner life and the need to care for it. Exercises are undertaken to control and ultimately transform the turmoil of the mind into a state of calm clarity within which a new sense of self—the silent self—can emerge. We need not wait for this to be fully achieved (if we did, we would wait forever) in order to begin meditating on the sublime thoughts of scripture, the mysteries of nature, on our own human constitution, or the research issues with which we are struggling. Finally, we must journey back to life as a fully incarnated being, integrating our contemplative experiences into life, grateful for the time and experiences we have been given, and cognizant that our work in life will be enriched by them. Each day we begin again the patient work of renewal. As Thoreau wrote, "They say that characters were engraven on the bathing tub of King Tching-thang to this effect: 'Renew thyself completely each day; do it again, and again, and forever again.'"[32]

---

32. Thoreau, *Walden and Civil Disobedience*, p. 60.

CHAPTER TWO

Discovering the Door

The doorway leading to the territory of contemplative practice is always there unobtrusively ready, but we do need to turn away from the relentless thrust of life and open it. The fifteenth-century mathematician, philosopher, and cardinal Nicholas of Cusa kept a simple hermit's cell ready for his arrival at the Benedictine Abbey of Tegernsee, where he acted as spiritual director. However, as a valued diplomat, he was sent by the Pope on a never-ending series of missions, which he dutifully fulfilled. Cusa understandably longed to complement his active life in service to his church with an equally active life of meditation and prayer in service of his soul. After every journey Cusa planned to retreat to his hermitage, but he never managed it. The demands of ecclesiastical life were unrelenting. The hermit's cell remained ready but unvisited.

Many today share Cusa's longing. Even though we do not need a hermit's cell to begin the work of meditative practice, it may prove as difficult for us to find the time to meditate as it was for Nicholas of Cusa. A surprising number of hindrances arise as one approaches meditation. Some obstacles are of our own manufacture, while others beset us from without with the persistence of the Furies keeping us from having a moment of peace or solitude. In the morning the day's demands quickly crowd in; at night, exhausted, we sit down to meditate and succeed only in falling asleep. We may have difficulty finding the right way to start meditating, and once we settle down our mental day-planner pops up with an urgent reminder, cutting short our reverie. To cap it all off the phone rings at exactly the moment when we are having our first success. Is it any wonder

that Cusa yearned for his remote hermitage? Each of these challenges—
inner and outer—must be met and mastered in order to establish a meditative life. As attractive as the hermit's cell may be, modern life requires
that we establish our practice in the midst of our daily obligations.

The contrast between our lives and those of monks could hardly be
greater. The medieval monk largely abandoned worldly life by entering
the cloister. In this regard consider a passage from the book of religious
instruction *The Imitation of Christ*, written in 1441 by Thomas à Kempis:
"Turn to the Lord with your whole heart, and forsake this wretched
world: your soul shall find rest. Learn to despise outward things, and to
give yourself to inward things: you shall see the Kingdom of God come
within you."[33] Whereas Thomas and his fellow Brothers of the Common
Life could devote their lives to the monastic duties of scriptural study,
prayer, and meditation, we live and work in a realm that is a blend of the
secular and the sacred. This new geometry of life is, I believe, an essential
factor shaping modern spiritual practice. When properly undertaken, the
meditative life renews and enlivens us, equipping us all the more for life.
Indeed, I will repeatedly suggest that we can learn to discover the sacred
in the secular. Instead of fleeing from "this wretched world" we learn to
approach it with a deeper appreciation, and if we possess a well-schooled
eye and open heart we can uncover in "outward things" the kingdom and
the peace that Thomas sought in "inward things" alone.

Having discovered the doorway of contemplative life, let us step inside.
As I hope is now clear, the passageway does not lead us away from life but
into it with greater vitality, compassion, and clarity of mind. Our first steps
along the path concern how we might best attend to the interior through
the cultivation of humility, reverence, and an openness to the unexpected.

Attending to the Interior

Meditation is a schooling for experiencing life from the inside. As important as the exterior aspects of life are, an equally important but largely

---

33. Thomas à Kempis, *The Imitation of Christ*, trans. Abbot Justin McCann (New York:
New American Library, 1957), Book 2, Chapter 1, p. 52.

silent component of reality resides behind the easy exteriority of things. Most of our lives are relentlessly committed to the external necessities and pleasures of life. Our jobs and families, our travel and entertainment, figure prominently in the turn of the seasons and the hours of the day. These diverse aspects are automatically experienced from the outside; it takes conscious effort to experience life from the inside. Every outside has an inside, but that inside goes largely unobserved.

Imagine that half the world is hidden from you. Half of the person sitting across from you has never been appreciated, half of the garden has never been seen or smelled, half of your own life has never been truly witnessed and appraised. If we fail to attend to the interior of self and world then, indeed, half the world is missed. When we turn toward contemplation we are turning to the forgotten half, toward that half of the world which modestly and patiently awaits our freely given attention. While the rest of the world is on red alert, shouting for every minute of our conscious life, the equally important interior dimensions of existence wait quietly. When it seems impossible to find the time to meditate, we can remind ourselves of these facts. We give so much time to the demands of the world; isn't it proper and even essential to give time to the silent half of the world that patiently waits us? Shouldn't we give as much time to the inner as we do to the outer?

With such thoughts we recall that the good we do has a source. Are we not profoundly nourished and guided by the inner dimensions of existence? Can we really know and do good if we are cut off from the gentle interior source of renewal and wisdom? We can be guided by outer tradition, but aren't the great wisdom traditions themselves grounded in that same interior realm? As our world increases in complexity I grow more and more convinced that it has become imperative for us to find our own original relationship to that luminous well and not to rely on tradition alone.

Every time I read the opening lines of Ralph Waldo Emerson's 1836 essay *Nature*, I hear the voice of one pleading for us to attend to the deepest aspects of the world, and not rely only on reports from our forefathers, no matter how wise. Emerson is not admonishing us to turn away from the world or to forget the past, but rather to see reality for ourselves and to see it whole.

Why should not we also enjoy an original relation to the universe? Why should not we have a poetry and philosophy of insight and not of tradition, and a religion by revelation to us, and not the history of theirs?... The sun shines to-day also. There is more wool and flax in the fields.[34]

Perhaps it was once enough to be faithful and to follow the dictums of church and state, but now we must find the wool and flax in today's fields ourselves. The sun does indeed shine on and into us as well as on our forefathers.

Finally, after thirty-five years of practice the true force of meditation is well known to me. I feel its unambiguous presence, or occasionally its absence, in my life. Stop physical exercise, and is there any doubt as to the consequences? The practice and cessation of meditation leave equally compelling evidence in the mental and moral life of the practitioner. When the press of life threatens to thwart my turning to the interior, these are the thoughts that bring me back to it again and again. Attending to the interior is like turning to a meal that has been prepared by invisible friends who await the guest regardless of whether he or she ever shows up. The table is always set, the banquet ready, but whether we remember to attend is up to us. The hospitality of our invisible companions deserves our response. We and others can only benefit by living a whole life, one that integrates both halves of existence, one that is nourished by both sources—interior and exterior.

Tirelessly, Rumi reminds us of the silent call to turn from our preoccupation with the small externalities of our lives—the "little figurines"—and to discover the artist within each of us. Once we have discovered the door, we take up the great work.

> Forget your life. *Say God is Great.* Get up.
> You think you know what time it is. It's time to pray.
> You've carved so many little figurines, too many...
> Tomorrow you'll see what you've broken and torn tonight,

---

34. Ralph Waldo Emerson, *Nature* (1836), *Selected Essays*, edited by Larzer Ziff (New York: Penguin Books, 1982), p. 35.

thrashing in the dark. Inside you
there's an artist you don't know about.
He's not interested in how things look different in moonlight.[35]

Rhythm, Tempo, and Posture

The external aspects of meditation—when and how often to meditate, the appropriate length of the session, proper posture, and what I call the "tempo" of meditation—are less lofty but significant. Let's take these up immediately.

Mornings and evenings are excellent times to meditate, and each has its own character, inviting us to vary the practice in accord with the time of day. In the morning we are moving from sleep into a wakeful engagement with life, and we can make use of this fact in meditation. Conversely, in the evening we have concluded our day's activity and are transitioning to sleep. We should be mindful of this difference. An invigorating meditation at night, for example, can lighten our sleep significantly or cause problematic insomnia. Meditating at both times of day is beneficial but certainly not essential. Later in the book I will give practices suited to these different times of day.

Rhythm and regularity are enormously helpful, and indeed later become an essential part of the practice. Miss your morning coffee and you get a caffeine-induced headache. Your body grows to expect the stimulation of coffee at a particular time each day, so if you skip the coffee, your body reacts. Our psyche can become equally attuned to the rather more constructive rhythms of meditative life. By living within these rhythms we strengthen and build the inner life. By contrast, a chaotic and disorderly practice leads to an inner dynamic that is conflicted and confused. These considerations are of particular importance if one has succeeded in establishing a strong and sustained meditative practice. Disorder that suddenly enters into an otherwise solid practice can be quite disturbing. By contrast, at the outset, any time given to meditation is time well spent. As the practice builds and strengthens it becomes increasingly important

---

35. *The Enlightened Heart*, ed. Stephen Mitchell, trans. Coleman Barks with A. J. Arberry (New York: Harper & Row, 1989), p. 56.

to find a time that is most likely to be available each day, and to maintain the rhythm of practice you have established.

The duration of meditation can be as short as five minutes or as long as an hour, or indeed more. On some occasions one is working within outer constraints, in other cases one is not time-limited. Adjust the meditation accordingly. In the language of chapter one, I always find my way to the door of humility and the path of reverence as a minimum. If I have time then I add inner hygiene exercises designed to support my psychological well-being for at least a few minutes, and then again, time permitting, I add a brief meditation on a verse or image. If I have a longer period available I take more time at each phase of the meditation, and use my inner sense of time to guide me in how much effort to give to each part of the practice. Usually it becomes clear inwardly whether one is finished or should press on a bit longer.

One cannot meditate *fast*. It is simply impossible. As a consequence, if you have only five minutes, spend it on a single aspect of the entire practice. Hurrying is antithetical to the required tempo of meditation. The tempo of meditation is the tempo of the arts. Consider, for example, the following Emily Dickinson poem. Read these lines as fast as you can:

> I many times thought peace had come,
> When peace was far away;
> As wrecked men deem they sight the land
> At centre of the sea,
>
> And struggle slacker, but to prove,
> As hopelessly as I,
> How many fictitious shores
> Before the harbor lie.

Did you feel an inner resistance to speeding through the words? Now read them much more slowly and aloud, savoring the sounds and meanings. In the second way we experience the artistry of the poem. Its beauty is revealed through cadence, imagery, tone, and content. Poetry demands that we respect its time-organism. When reading fast, you may understand the lines but the artistry is inaccessible, the time-organism is violated, the poem is dead. Thought can move at lightning speed, but the art of the poem demands a slower tempo, the tempo of heartbeat and breath, the tempo of life and feeling. Whether beholding a painting or listening to music, whether reading poetry or viewing a play, time must slow down in order for us to enter into the object of our attention with our heart as well as our head. If our thinking runs along with the worries of the day, or presses too forcefully, we remain outside the art of the painting, poetry, or performance. Likewise, if we try to meditate "fast" we remain outside the meditation, performing the mental actions but with none of the requisite feelings and perceptions. In this sense, meditation is an art.

The relationship of meditation to tempo is clearly of deep significance. In one lecture Rudolf Steiner indicated that in order for us to awaken to the spiritual aspects of existence we need to bring cognition—normally associated with the rapidity of thinking—to the more measured tempo of heartbeat and breath.[36] This is one reason why the Asian traditions made use of the breath as a focus for meditation. While Steiner generally shunned breathing meditation, he emphasized the importance of a slower tempo for meditative practice and cognition. The point is not to focus on a bodily process such as breathing, but to transform the way we know so that the tempo of the breath is the tempo of cognition. A few slow, deep breaths at the beginning of a practice session can work wonders in slowing our rhythm of attention and releasing stress. Set aside multi-tasking and the acceleration of life. Embrace the graceful, poetic rhythms of artistic attention and your meditation will gradually grow and flower.

It is not necessary to assume a special posture in order to meditate. Your posture should support the practice, simultaneously encouraging mental alertness and inner repose. Sitting comfortably on the edge of a bed or chair with feet on the ground and back upright, hands on the thighs or resting in the lap, is a good way to begin. One can stand or even lie down, but what is significant is that one feels supported by the posture.

---

36. Rudolf Steiner, *The Karma of Materialism*, trans. Rita Stebbing (Spring Valley, NY: Anthroposophic Press, 1985). See especially lectures of 7 and 14 August 1917. For example, "All the exercises described in the book *Knowledge of Higher Worlds and Its Attainment* are the spiritual correlate suited to the West, of that for which the Orient longs: to bring the rhythm of the process of breathing into the process of cognition. If our thinking had the same tempo as our breathing many secrets of the universe would be disclosed to us" (p. 36).

Body-based Contemplative Practice

Perhaps the most common form of contemplative practice in America today is meditative movement, by which I mean yoga, Tai Chi, and other movement practices. While of value in their own right, such body-based practices can also be a useful entry point for contemplative practice in general. They offer the practitioner a physical rather than a purely mental way to school attention, and can act as an important prelude to sitting meditation.

More than the other practices described in this book, body-based meditation is best learned in person and will not be described here. Some instructors, in addition to working with physical postures, also guide the student to the accompanying inner moods and modes of attention that such movements evoke. I should make clear that in this instance one is not interested in exercise primarily for the purpose of physical fitness or weight loss. These may be worthy goals, but the purpose of body-based meditation is to bring us from the outward orientation of conventional life to the more deliberate tempo and inner orientation of contemplative life.

In recent years I have made use of certain therapeutic eurythmy gestures that are recommended as especially helpful to everyone.[37] I have found these meditative movements to be wonderfully supportive as part of my morning meditation. They precede everything else I do, bringing me into an enlivened and centered state of awareness. Body-based meditative movement is an excellent way to begin practice.

Contemplative Community

Meditation is largely a solitary enterprise. Yet, as I have already mentioned, in a variety of ways we can be supported in meditation through others. Perhaps the simplest way is to attend a meditation workshop or retreat. The instruction, the practice sessions, the conversation concerning obstacles, all bring encouragement and clarification. Our personal problems

---

37. Eurythmy is an art of movement inaugurated by Lori Smits under Rudolf Steiner's direction, which also has wide therapeutic application.

are often common to many others, and those that are unique to us can generally be addressed privately.

During retreats individuals often comment that contemplative practice is much easier and goes deeper than when practicing alone. My own experience confirms this. I see this as both a benefit that we can use, and also as a danger of which we should be aware. It is a benefit because we experience the power and reality of the contemplative mind during the retreat; we sense real inner development during a short period and so are encouraged. Conversely, when we are alone we may feel inadequate and distracted, and long for the group. Dependency on the group is a danger. The instruction we received during the retreat was intended to strengthen us, to make us more fully human as individuals. While this certainly includes the appreciation of others, codependency is something quite different. The purpose of meditation is not to create retreat junkies, but to transform ourselves as individuals. This transformation depends on our personal effort, not on the magic of the instructor or of the group. With these caveats, a contemplative community can be a genuine support to the cultivation of the inner life, and we all can benefit by being part of one.

The wakefulness that results from contemplative practice can, when joined with inner equanimity and empathy, create the possibility for a new form of community life. Whereas traditional communities are based on shared ethnic, religious, or national identity, contemplative communities can be truly diverse, transcending such traditional bases for fellowship. With the birth of the silent self we step outside the particularities of our social self and become part of the human family. I would even say that our awareness can reach beyond the strictly human to experience our interconnectedness with all existence. If we are able to bring this level of awareness to each other, if we can listen from the center of our being and speak to the highest in the other, then a new kind of relationship is formed, one based in freedom. While honoring the unique specificity of our lives, it simultaneously reaches to that which connects us beyond difference. Such community life is extremely rare, but I feel that the future will increasingly ask it of us. The reality of interconnectedness must become a lived experience, and there is no better support for this awareness than contemplative practice.

Starting with Wonder

> *Climb the mountains and get their good tidings.*
>
> *Nature's peace will flow into you as sunshine flows*
>
> *into trees. The winds will blow their own freshness into*
>
> *you, and the storms their energy, while cares will drop*
>
> *off like autumn leaves.*
>
> — JOHN MUIR, *Our National Parks*, 1901[38]

Nature's peace can stream into us like sunshine flowing into trees, and faced with her grandeur our cares can drop like autumn leaves. John Muir's experience in the wilderness areas of America can be replicated in every coppice of trees, along any stream or seashore. Nature can be of great help in fostering the mood of humility and reverence that is so essential as the foundation for contemplative practice. We need not be in the wilderness in order to cultivate the mood she can bestow. Instead one can imagine a natural landscape, making it the focus for our contemplative attention. From the star-strewn night sky, a wide expanse of coastline, a deer grazing, or a mountain view can arise all we require. The scene we choose, real or imagined, is a means of evoking a felt sense of presence beyond the mundane. Through it we shift our attention from daily affairs to the enduring and essential aspect of things. We feel drawn to a deep stillness beyond self or personal concerns, and into a mode of awareness that supports further contemplative work.

Edmund Burke wrote of the "sublime" as that which could cause wonder, reverence, terror, and astonishment in us. In it we sense the infinite in the finite and are drawn out and beyond our smaller selves to sample that unending expanse. Time slows or even stops as we settle into the sky, sea, or mountain. In Burke's words, "The passion caused by the great and

---

38. John Muir, *Our National Parks* (Boston: Houghton Mifflin, 1901) p. 56.

sublime in nature is astonishment, and astonishment is that state of the soul in which all its motions are suspended."[39] This is one way we can enter into the mood suited for meditation. By simply attending inwardly to nature, by allowing it to lead us into stillness, peace, and wonder, by opening to its transcendent presence, in these ways we discover the portal of humility and the path of reverence that prepare us for meditation.

One can linger long within the precincts of nature and notice that astonishment changes and deepens in us as we sustain the mood. This was brought home to me through an experience I had in, of all places, a luxury office atop the Rockefeller Center in Manhattan. I was working for a foundation at the time and was participating in a meeting between environmental activists and the major foundations that supported them. The meeting was chaired by Maurice Strong who had been the secretary-general of the Earth Summit in Rio in 1992. The conversation was vigorous, with the environmentalists making well-reasoned and passionate cases for the programs they believed would mitigate the problems we face. On the other side of the table we funders pondered how their suggestions would fit into our own funding guidelines and priorities, and what our boards of directors would think of the proposals. At the far end of the table sat a long-haired, dark-skinned man in a flannel shirt and jeans. He was quietly following the proceedings with downcast eyes. After we had been at it for quite a while, Maurice's wife, Hanna, said that perhaps now would be a good time to hear from the man at her side. He stood up and began to sing in a language I had never heard, but that seemed to stretch back to the beginnings of time. I felt as if our previous debates were suddenly placed against a vast moral backdrop. They seemed somehow puny, for all their passion and reason. Here was the cry of lived experience, and in the words he spoke afterwards, the suffering of the Earth was given fresh expression. It was a language that spoke of the Ancestors whose bones and blood were mingled with Mother Earth; it spoke of a spiritual relationship to the Earth that was primary, uninterrupted, and incontestable. In that moment my own funding priorities

---

39. Edmund Burke, *On the Sublime and Beautiful*, Part II, Section 1 (New York: Harper, 1844), p. 11.

were set.[40] Here was a voice that not only wondered at nature's beauties but knew her soul as well. It said, "The Earth was and is our Mother. She is alive, her sufferings are real, and you are her children and stewards."

Far away from John Muir's wilderness I felt a shift. My experience changed from astonishment at nature's grandeur to a sense of the moral agency that animates her. In that moment my attitude also changed fundamentally from awe to reverence. The native peoples of all continents live within a tradition that fosters an awareness of the sacred being of nature and therefore a reverence before her. Our environmental groups largely lack the consciousness of the Earth as Mother; we have much to learn from our indigenous brothers and sisters in this regard. In deepening our relationship to nature by moving from wonder and awe to reverence, we meet nature not as a physical mechanism but as a moral and spiritual agent. While science will protest that we are merely projecting our moral inclinations onto nature, we can inwardly sense the emptiness of that assertion. Every civilization except ours has understood that we are not the only moral agents in the universe. Our survival depends on setting aside such self-centeredness and acknowledging the agential or "being" character of the world around us. It is then possible to feel true reverence toward nature, our fellow human beings, and towards those beings or Being who have always been active within her.

In our meditative practice we can cultivate the above change in consciousness. For example, consider a still mountain pond surrounded by stone and trees. Birds wing across the pond, and an occasional fish breaks its surface. The blue sky and white clouds are reflected in its depths. Sitting with such an image, we can recognize at least four stages on the path of reverence.[41] We first meet the pond with *wonder*. Before the sublime we are astonished by what we experience, we are awed and quietly amazed, joy spreads through us, and we are simultaneously energized and settled

---

40. The meeting resulted in an initiative with a group of Native American spiritual leaders who approached the difficult question of Mother Earth Spirituality and Sustainable Development.

41. Rudolf Steiner, *The World of the Senses, World of the Spirit*, translator not given (London: Rudolf Steiner Press, 1947) Lecture 1, December 27, 1911. See also "The Mission of Reverence," *The Metamorphosis of the Soul* trans. C. Davy and C. von Arnim (London: Rudolf Steiner Press, 1983) Vol. 1, Oct 28, 1909.

inwardly. Wonder can change to *reverence* when we ponder the force or agency that lies behind the phenomenon beheld. As in a work of art, we recognize the wisdom and beauty that are reflected in the form, colors, sounds, and movements of the mountain pond. How did these come into existence? What wise and generous agency created them? No longer an "It," that which is before us has become a "Thou," in Martin Buber's language.[42] In the third stage we find ourselves drawn more and more deeply into the scene of pond and mountain. We resound with the interior tones and currents of that which is before us. Its own harmonious nature sounds also in us. We *participate* in the pond, sensing its watery nature; we live partly into the hard stone that rises up on all sides, we open into the infinite reaches of the sky. Our own sense of autonomy and identity blurs and we identify increasingly with the other. The Thou before us moves gradually into us. The final stage is *self-surrender*. The universal, protean aspect of our own nature is capable of becoming all things, and in the final fourth stage we do exactly this. Subject-object consciousness disappears and a non-dual form of awareness takes its place. We know from within because we are the object itself.

Albert Schweitzer recounts his discovery of reverence as a guide while making his way by boat along the narrow creeks of Africa. He tells us that he was seeking a universal ground for ethics, writing his reflection in his journal as he traveled. Suddenly, "Late on the third day, at the very moment when, at sunset, we were making our way through a herd of hippopotamuses, there flashed upon my mind, unforeseen and unsought, the phrase, 'Reverence for Life.' The iron door had yielded: the path in the thicket had become visible." Reverence opened a path for Schweitzer as it can for us.

The closing lines of Mary Oliver's poem "Wild Geese" reminds us, "Whoever you are, no matter how lonely, / the world offers itself to your imagination, / calls to you like the wild geese, harsh and exciting—/ over and over announcing your place / in the family of things."[43] Schweitzer

---

42. Martin Buber, *I and Thou*, trans. Walter Kaufmann (New York: Charles Scribner's Sons, 1970).

43. Mary Oliver, "Wild Geese," *Dream Work* (New York: Atlantic Monthly Press, 1986), p. 14.

heard the call. The world's offer is one we should take up repeatedly. When we are open enough it will surely awaken us to a true ethic based on a reverence for life.

Whether experienced by Thoreau on Walden Pond, or John Muir writing on the Western wilderness, or Mary Oliver musing on wild geese, nature continuously invites us to move beyond our physical and psychological struggles and to enter into a vaster universal rhythm and current that embraces us always but mostly remains unnoted. It offers itself to our imagination, calls to us, announcing our place within the family of things. We have evolved in relationship with these currents of nature, and we can use them as a trusted foundation for our meditative life every day of our lives.

Openness to the Unexpected

Prayer does not change God,

but it changes him who prays.

— SØREN KIERKEGAARD

In his novel *Les Misérables* Victor Hugo wrote, "Certain thoughts are prayers. There are moments when, whatever the attitude of the body, the soul is on its knees."[44] Certain thoughts, if we allow them their full force, do move us to reflections and moods that humble us—they figuratively bring us to our knees. For many individuals today, however, traditional prayer is simply not possible. They may lack a connection to it or even feel a strong negative association. Yet throughout history and in all cultures, prayer has been the single greatest means used in the cultivation of a religious life. This is as true of the Native peoples of North America and the ancient religions of the Near East as it is of the religions of Asia and Africa. For those who can pray, it is a long-honored way to humility and reverence.

---

44. Victor Hugo, *Les Misérables*, Book V, Chapter 4.

Most individuals who wish to use prayer as a starting point for their meditative practice do so out of a particular religious tradition, and select a prayer from that tradition to use as the entry point. The prayer may be recited silently or aloud, but in all cases with full attention to the words and thoughts spoken. As with the tempo of poetry, we slowly and patiently live into the words and thoughts of the prayer as completely as possible. If distracted, we can always return to a line and repeat it. Gradually our mood changes and we sense the effects of the prayer on us. We welcome the change and make space for it. We recognize the reorientation toward the sacred, and our inner posture becomes one of modest devotion, the proper foundation for the meditative life.

Consider a prayer from each of four traditions. I begin with a prayer of the Sioux people of the upper Plains region of what today is the United States and Canada. In it the Sun is first heard and then seen bringing joy and light to the beings of the Earth. That light in turn is offered back to Wakan-Tanka or the Great Spirit by the one who prays.

> The Sun, the Light of the world,
> I hear Him coming.
> I see his face as He comes.
> He makes the beings on earth happy.
> And they rejoice.
> O Wakan-Tanka, I offer to You this world of Light.[45]

This prayer begins with the recognition of the greatness of the world, its blessings and life. The Sun is not considered scientifically, but is addressed as He whose face can be seen and whose journey can be heard. The gift of light granted by the Sun to humanity is not hoarded but passed on to the Great Spirit worshiped by the Sioux. The gifts we receive are not ours but reside with us only until we discover Him to whom the gift should next be given. In prayers such as this we inwardly present ourselves before the world and a being far greater than ourselves; we humble ourselves before them and appreciate with profound gratitude what they offer us. And what we receive, we give away; we cultivate the spirit of generosity.

---

45. These prayers are taken from www.worldprayers.org.

In many world religions the Sun, the giver of light, is an image or symbol of the divine. Halfway around the world, the practitioners of the solar religion of Zoroastrianism recite the Gathas of Zarathustra, which also celebrate the Sun viewed as the divine spirit Ahura Mazda. They seek his aid in revealing Truth and Wisdom.

> So may we be like those making
> the world progress toward perfection;
> May Mazda and the Divine Spirits help us
> and guide our efforts through Truth;
> For a thinking man is where Wisdom is at home.

We are on a journey; the prayer petitions Mazda for help in guiding us to join those whose actions lead the world toward perfection. This noble work is not performed alone but with the help of Divine Spirits. When thoughts such as these are uttered with sincerity, the petitioner inwardly turns from the concerns of daily life toward the doorway of practice and the journey that ensues. As with the Sioux prayer, we recognize that the human being is part of a larger order in which we can participate and before which we should be humble and devout.

Closer to home, consider the thirteenth-century prayer of St. Francis of Assisi.

> Lord, make me an instrument of Thy peace;
> where there is hatred, let me sow love;
> where there is injury, pardon;
> where there is doubt, faith;
> where there is despair, hope;
> where there is darkness, light;
> and where there is sadness, joy.
>
> O Divine Master,
> grant that I may not so much seek to be consoled as to console;
> to be understood, as to understand;
> to be loved, as to love;
> for it is in giving that we receive,

it is in pardoning that we are pardoned,
and it is in dying that we are born to eternal life.
Amen.

Whenever I read the prayer of St. Francis I am reminded of the words of the eighth-century Indian Buddhist scholar Shantideva, who practiced and taught the bodhisattvic way of life.

> May I be a protector to those without protection,
> A leader for those who journey,
> And a boat, a bridge, a passage
> For those desiring the further shore.
>
> May the pain of every living creature
> Be completely cleared away.
> May I be the doctor and the medicine
> And may I be the nurse
> For all sick beings in the world
> Until everyone is healed.
>
> Just like space
> And the great elements such as earth,
> May I always support the life
> Of all the boundless creatures.
>
> And until they are released from pain
> May I also be the source of life
> For all the realms of varied beings
> That reach unto the ends of space.

Although on different continents and separated by centuries, St. Francis and Shantideva voiced the same sentiments. They sought to become healing forces in a world of illness and suffering; they sought to console and support all those in need. The teaching of love was lived by both, and by the millions who followed their teaching. They prayed as an affirmation and reminder of their commitment. That he might not waver in his efforts, Francis sought support from God. As a Buddhist, Shantideva did not address himself to a god because his was a non-theistic religion, but he petitioned nonetheless asking, "May I be a protector…" Even here the one who prays reaches beyond the self to that which is greater than the individual. The inner mood is humility; the gesture is that of love and service.

Those who have a positive relationship to prayer can find in it another doorway into meditation. No matter how experienced one is in contemplative practice, prayer is of benefit. When one sits down in order to practice, prayer offers a way to ignite the spark of sacred attention that meditation will fan into a flame.[46] We will look further at this process, including the contemplative religious practice known as "centering prayer," in chapter five.

In all traditions of meditation, moral preparation is preliminary to everything else. All other dimensions of the practice rest on this foundation, and it is therefore imperative to make it secure through preliminary contemplative exercises in which the fundamental moods are cultivated by prayer or through nature meditation. Moreover, we are never done with this part of the practice. Throughout life's long walk the moral

---

46. I take this image from Rudolf Steiner's lecture *Prayer*, February 17, 1910, translated by Henry Monges (New York: Anthroposophic Press, 1966). In this lecture Steiner speaks of the significance of prayer at all stages of spiritual development. He regularly used the following adaptation of the Lord's Prayer himself.

> Father, You who were, are, and will be in our inmost being,
> May your name be glorified and praised in us.
> May your kingdom grow in our deeds and inmost lives.
> May we perform your will as you, Father, lay it down
>   in our inmost being.
> You give us spiritual nourishment, the bread of life,
>   superabundantly in all the changing conditions of our lives.
> Let our mercy toward others make up for the sins done to our being.
> You do not allow the tempter to work in us beyond the capacity of our strength.
> For no temptation can live in your being, Father,
> and the tempter is only appearance and delusion, from which you lead us,
> Father, through the light of knowledge.
> May your power and glory work in us through all periods and ages of time.
> Amen. [translation by Christopher Bamford]

foundations of the meditative life require regular attention, so we should include prayer or reverence before nature in our daily practice. Doing so sanctifies the way before us and makes it bright with the glory of the divine.

> With beauty before me, I walk.
> With beauty behind me, I walk.
> With beauty above me, I walk.
> With beauty below me, I walk.
> With beauty all around me, I walk.
>   Navajo Night Chant

Openness to the Unexpected

> *A philosopher asked Buddha:*
>
> *"Without words, without silence,*
>
> *will you tell me the truth?"*
>
> — Zen kōan

Nicholas of Cusa once composed a small but exquisite book, *The Vision of God*, for his monastic brethren in which he recommended an unusual contemplative exercise. Together with the manuscript Cusa sent his monks a portrait of the Christ painted in such a way that the eyes of the figure followed the viewer. He then suggested that the monks hang the painting in the refectory, and that they go in twos to view the painting. The monks were to stand on opposite sides of the large room. Each monk would experience the figure as looking at them, a strange situation to contemplate. Then, Cusa asked, the monks should walk towards one another reflecting all the while that the single pair of painted eyes not only were following him but also were simultaneously following his companion—an impossible fact. Cusa termed this the "coincidence of opposites." The exercise was designed to break the tyranny of logical thinking (or *ratio*) schooled on sensate reality in order to prepare the student for another and higher mode of experiential knowing he termed *intellectus* or *visio*, the vision of God.

Within the Zen tradition, the pupil would be given a kōan like the one that opens this section as a means of challenging his conventional intellect. Ekai, also called Mumon, compiled a collection of 48 kōans called *The Gateless Gate*. In one of them Kyogen says: "Zen is like a man hanging in a tree by his teeth over a precipice. His hands grasp no branch, his feet rest on no limb, and under the tree another person asks him: 'Why does Bodhidharma come to China from India?' If the man in tree does not answer, he fails; and if he does answer, he falls and loses his life. Now what shall he do?" The point is not to reason to a correct answer but to live the dilemma. Resolution arises at a different level of awareness from that immediately brought to bear.

Like Ekai's, Cusa's exercise was intended as preparation for the transition from one domain of experience to another. The doorway approached through meditation is a threshold separating two spaces, or, perhaps better said, two aspects of our one undivided reality. Our habitual ways of experiencing and understanding, while essential to conventional life, prove inadequate and even an obstacle to experience and understanding in the new domain associated with meditation. As we move toward the doorway of meditative experience, we need to undertake the difficult task of setting aside our habitual expectations generated in the sense world and look with fresh eyes and an open mind.

In a famous Platonic allegory, a prisoner is released from a cave where he and his fellows have been confined from childhood. They have seen nothing of the world outside, and all their reality has consisted of shadows on the cavern walls. The freed man climbs through the long passage, breaking out into the light outside the cave. Blinded by the light, he needs time to make out what is around him, and longer still to understand it. When he returns home, back into the cave, his reports are met with disbelief and ridicule. The experiences of meditative life can indeed be difficult to capture in conventional language or concepts. Yet, to those who have lived them, their reality and force are not diminished in the least by this fact. Especially at the outset we should refrain from trying to understand them with the conventional perspective of sense-born logic. We can acknowledge the experience and allow uncertainty as to its meaning. An attitude of openness to the unexpected is appropriate.

Like Nicholas of Cusa, Rudolf Steiner described this difficulty by contrasting sense-based logic with an intelligence that is more like seeing.

> This has to do with the fact that it is only on the physical plane that we can use concepts.... Yet, what can be clearly and necessarily linked together through concepts on the physical plane immediately changes as soon as we enter the neighboring supersensible world. Thus we see that two worlds interpenetrate; one of them can be grasped with concepts and the other cannot, but can only be perceived.[47]

The laws of cause and effect, the logic of the machine world, so familiar to us in ordinary experience, are no longer appropriate as we move into those domains that open to us through meditation. Are truly human actions such as forgiveness and selfless love bound by the laws of cause and effect? Some might argue so, but they are mistaken. Yes, much in our lives is determined by outer causes or driven by psychological necessity. But within this dense domain of law, freedom also extends its gentle hand. We need not be driven by hatred or greed; in fact, the more we resist the simple biological imperatives of behavior, the more human we become. In meditation we approach the region of freedom. Therefore the rigid laws of logic based on material existence are replaced by what we might term a logic of being or agency. At the threshold of such a realm we are bound to confront a "coincidence of opposites." Like Cusa's monks we should practice sustaining the opposites, even leveraging them, delighting in their sheer impossibility. Only by learning their language will we learn the language of freedom. Only by learning to perceive (*visio*) will we come to knowledge in the domain opened to us through meditation.

Doorways always connect adjacent rooms from two sides. In other words, when we end our meditation we should do so consciously, passing back again through the door in the direction leading to embodied reality with all its practical demands. When waking up to the dawn we

---

47. Rudolf Steiner, *Necessity and Freedom*, January 25, 1916, trans. Pauline Wehrle (Hudson, NY: Anthroposophic Press, 1988) p. 21.

return to our daily obligations refreshed by our nightly journey. Likewise the fruits of our meditation can and should be bundled and taken into life. However, if at the end of a meditation session we fail to return with conscious intent, neglecting to seal the practice session with gratitude, then the danger arises that we will carry the meditative state into life and dream our way through it. Nothing we do or experience in our contemplative life should lead us from the world or toward irresponsible action. Quite the contrary, the suffering of others, the needs of the world, become all the more pressing, and we rise to meet the call with increasing wisdom and strength. Meditation should never take us away from life, but should rather equip us all the better to meet its demands. Crossing the threshold of the doorway properly in both directions assures openness to the unexpected gifts of spirit, but also firms our resolve to be active and compassionate in life.

Like so many other poets, Rumi calls us to wakefulness at the great round and open doorsill of the sacred life.

> The breeze at dawn has secrets to tell you.
> Don't go back to sleep.
> You must ask for what you really want.
> Don't go back to sleep.
> People are going back and forth across the doorsill
> where the two worlds touch.
> The door is round and open.
> Don't go back to sleep.[48]

---

48. Rumi, from *The Essential Rumi*, trans. Coleman Barks with John Moyne (San Francisco: Harper San Francisco, 1995), p. 36.

CHAPTER THREE

Finding Peace, Cultivating Wakefulness

Is my soul asleep?...

No, my soul is not asleep.

It is awake, wide awake.

It neither sleeps nor dreams, but watches,

Its eyes wide open

to far-off things, and listens

at the shores of the great silence.[49]

— ANTONIO MACHADO

A social-worker friend has described to me a frequent reaction she gets after counseling her clients to take a few deep breaths and to make some time for silence. They react strongly, saying, "No, thank you, I'm not going there!" In Machado's language, when we turn our step toward "the shores of the great silence" we all can experience timidity and even fear. Fear induces avoidance and self-distraction, which easily deflect us from the quiet and difficult work of self-knowledge. Yet if we are to be our

---

49. Antonio Machado, in *The Soul Is There for Its Own Joy*, ed. Robert Bly (Hopewell, NJ: Ecco Press, 1995), p. 29.

true selves, and if we are to serve with the best of who we are, then we cannot evade the shyness and fear we naturally feel when we confront the open interior space of stillness. Life's outer exuberance, in which we rightly delight, presses us with a thousand sights and sounds, which can be opportunities for insight as well as the occasion for complete distraction. But having succeeded in turning from them in meditation, having pushed past our anxieties and settled the body, we discover that the mind itself is an unruly place. We may have left the sensory tumult behind, but we have brought the mental tumult with us. Part of contemplative practice is, therefore, the care we give to ourselves in search of deep inner peace, supplanting the tumult with a quiet, open joy that patiently awaits all things.

In my experience, internal disturbances fall into two broad categories: uncontrolled thoughts and disquieting emotions. Beyond these two immediate problems is a third factor that works against success in meditation: inner laziness. We will need to confront languor as well. Once we have laid the moral foundation for meditation through the practices described in the previous chapter, we quickly discover the need to improve our ability to attend, strengthen our resolve, and stabilize our emotional life. I think of this as *inner hygiene*, which is as important for our inner life as physical hygiene is for our outer life. Rudolf Steiner recommends six exercises as a way of strengthening and balancing the practitioner's inner life. Michael Lipson has developed these in his book *Stairway of Surprise*.[50] The first three concern the care of thinking, willing, and feeling.

Strengthening Attention

In a sixteenth-century teaching tale a holy friar meets a ploughman whom the text describes as "all uplandish and rude."[51] The friar and

---

50. Rudolf Steiner, *Esoteric Development* (Spring Valley, NY: Anthroposophic Press, 1982), Chapter 5; Michael Lipson, *Stairway of Surprise* (Great Barrington, MA: SteinerBooks, 2002).
51. William Bonde, *The Pilgrim of Perfection* (London: W. de Worde, 1531), p. clx; quoted in Ross Fuller, *Brotherhood of the Common Life and its Influence* (Albany: SUNY Press, 1995), p. 244.

ploughman fall to debating the difficulties of holding a single thought without distraction. The ploughman claims that he can easily follow a train of thought without the slightest deviation. The holy father then challenges the ploughman, "Say one *Pater Noster* (Our Father) and think on no other thing, but only on that which you say and I shall give you my horse." The ploughman readily agrees. No sooner has he begun to say his prayer than his thoughts move him to ask, "If I succeed will I get the saddle and the bridle as well?"

Is your thinking your own? That is, do you direct your thinking or is it ruled by the random promptings of cell phones, doorbells, road signs, free-floating memories, associations, and so on? Observe your own thinking for a few minutes and you may well agree with a famous discussion of attention by the father of American psychology William James. He distinguished between active or voluntary attention and passive attention. "There is no such thing as voluntary attention sustained for more than a few seconds at a time," he declared.[52] That is, we may find ourselves engaged for some minutes by a fascinating thought, sports event, video game, or concert, but in all these cases our attention is riveted to the event not voluntarily but "passively." The inherent interest of the occurrence captures our attention. James felt that voluntary attention only lasts for a few seconds, usually to redirect our attention, which then resumes its passive character again once it is captured by the next interesting thought or event. Emily Dickinson described our plight this way:

> The thought behind I strove to join
>   Unto the thought before,
> But sequence raveled out of reach
>   Like balls upon a floor.[53]

Dickinson obviously knew her mind in more ways than one.

---

52. William James, *Principles of Psychology* (New York: H. Holt, 1890), Vol. 1, Chapter 11, p. 420.
53. Emily Dickinson, *Collected Poems of Emily Dickinson* (New York: Avenel Books, originally 1890). Original editions edited by Mabel Loomis Todd and T. W. Higginson, p. 35.

More recent experiments on attention have tended to confirm James's assertion. However, at a 2003 MIT conference of cognitive scientists and Buddhist monks/scholars, scientists were challenged to study expert meditators. Long-term Buddhist meditators claim the ability to sustain attention for minutes and even hours at a time.[54] In his book *The Bridge of Quiescence*, Alan Wallace presents a treatment of Buddhist meditation that is fully aware of the myriad obstacles to sustained attention, but maintains that these can be and have been overcome by some individuals who have undergone extensive mental training.[55] Wallace lays out the methods for cultivating sustained voluntary attention in lucid detail. And in 2007 Richard Davidson and colleagues reported research showing that the allocation of attentional resources can be changed through sustained meditation practice.[56] This suggests that William James's claim is correct for naïve subjects, but that voluntary attention can be schooled if we exert sufficient effort.

It is clear within all traditions, Eastern or Western, that initially our thoughts are not under our direction. Early on and throughout our practice it is, therefore, essential to school our thinking to come more and more under our control. The first exercise is aimed at the mastery of thinking and particularly of voluntary attention. Specifically, it is both revealing and helpful to concentrate on an extremely simple object such as a pin, paper clip, or pencil. The more insignificant the object, the better it serves the purposes of the exercise. Since the object lacks inherent interest, the attention we give it is entirely the result of our decision and effort.

First study the physical object carefully: its shape, color, size, structural components, etc. For example, if you have selected a paper clip, observe its shiny surface, the thickness of the wire of which it is made, its peculiar shape, and so on. Then close your eyes and imagine it before yourself in

---

54. Anne Harrington and Arthur Zajonc, *The Dalai Lama at MIT* (Cambridge: Harvard University Press, 2006).

55. B. Alan Wallace, *The Bridge of Quiescence* (Chicago: Open Court, 1998).

56. Heleene A. Shlagter, Antoine Lutz, Lawrence L. Greishar, Andrew D. Francis, Sander Nieuwenhuis, James M. David, and Richard J. Davidson "Mental Training Affects Distribution of Limited Brain Resources," *Public Library of Science: Biology*, June 2007, vol. 6, issue 6, e138.

detail. Can you call to mind the exact shape of the paper clip? If some aspects of the object elude you, go back to the physical object again and make further observations, repeating this until you have a clear mental picture of the whole object. Working now from the mental picture, turn the object over in your mind, and spend a minute or two carefully examining it in your mind's eye. Next you can consider its function. Mentally explore exactly how a paper clip holds several sheets of paper together. What must the qualities of the metal be in order to ensure a firm grasp and at the same time to leave essentially no marks on the papers? You can go on to picture the manufacturing process, the product's distribution, use, and so on. If your thoughts stray, as they certainly will, simply bring your attention back to the mental paper clip and pick up where you left off. The goal is to bring only observations and thoughts that are directly related to the paper clip or other simple object.

Five minutes of such practice each day will suffice to strengthen one's powers of concentration considerably. At the outset external distractions and mental digressions are constant; later, they are rare. The outer distractions disappear, for example, not because one has found a quiet place to practice but rather because of one's power of concentration. One learns to note the noise or other distraction briefly and return to the exercise, the noise taking on a background or secondary place in one's awareness. In his book on meditation the German theologian Friedrich Rittelmeyer goes so far as to suggest practicing in a noisy train station in order to intensify one's power of concentration. The distractions and digressions diminish because of a change in us.

Another means of handling external noise is to make it the subject of our attention. One can attend to the distraction fully, noting its particular character and tone, comparing it to other noises or distractions. In these ways either the external distractions are filtered out, or they are taken up and included in the exercise itself. This results in a new feeling of lucidity and fluidity in one's thinking. The ability to sustain attention voluntarily on an object of one's choice will be crucial to all subsequent forms of meditation. Therefore, although concentrating on a paper clip may seem an unlikely place to start, it is an essential step in learning to control one's thinking, and one that will be used repeatedly with more substantial practices.

One is never done with this practice, but should return to it often. It can become a regular feature of your daily practice. If over time your work on the paper clip becomes automatic, change to a new object. The only rule is that whatever you think must be connected closely to the object before you. Be disciplined but kind to yourself in this and in all practices. Apparent failure often precedes startling success.

Sustaining Resolve

Have you ever set your mind to something but failed to follow through? Have you had a brilliant idea but failed to execute it? Perhaps you know that an aspect of your behavior should change, or that a habit should be broken. You decide to read a particular book or write an important memo, only to put off the project for yet another day. The list of "shoulds" is discouragingly long. In everyday life, the ability to bring our intentions to full realization is crucial to success: so too with meditation. The intention to meditate is not good enough. In fact, everything we intend but fail to do undermines us. Better, therefore, to be realistic and to set attainable goals here as in all things. Undertake a practice only when you can realistically hope to execute it consistently. This need not discourage us from taking up meditation. We can begin with a very modest set of exercises, increasing the length and depth of practice over time. In addition, we can strengthen our will through particular exercises.

What we aim for in this case is the long commitment. The rhythm of the will is quite different from the rhythm of thinking. One thought can quickly follow the next. We can imagine an entire new life in an afternoon. Yet anything of significance in life requires years to accomplish. Thinking or fantasizing is quick and easy by comparison. Once we recognize the duration of the will, we can work at schooling it. We can set ourselves tasks that over time will allow us to actualize our intentions more consistently and over longer and longer periods without distraction. The second exercise aims at exactly these ends, and it will benefit us in both outer life and in our contemplative practice.

Choose a trivial action, one that you would be unlikely to do for any normal reason. At the same time each day, perform the action selected. It may be that you stand up and walk around your chair, or you spin the ring on your finger three times, and so on. The possibilities are endless. What is important is the consistency of action, not the action itself.

Another means of deepening the will entails bringing special attention to the normal actions of daily life. In the world of Buddhist mindfulness, Jon Kabat Zinn has made popular the conscious eating of a single raisin. Such attention can be given to any action we choose. So choose something: a short walk across the room, the drinking of your morning coffee, or the weeding of a single flowering rosebush. Slow the pace; attend to each intention and subsequent action. "Soften" the will so you enact each phase of the journey with receptivity. The world works back on you with each action of your own. Imagine that your work is part of a sacred ritual that is unknown to others, but which completes a large ceremonial composition. You morning coffee becomes a Japanese tea ceremony, your weeding a holy trust to care to the Earth. Each act is infused with artistry and meaning by being caught up in the imaginal, in story or myth.

A firm will is remarkably efficacious and can overcome apparently insurmountable adversity. The stories that most inspire are often those of human achievement against great odds, for example Helen Keller, who overcame blindness and deafness, or Ernest Shackleton, who led his crewmen to safety through seas of Antarctica and severe weather when all seemed lost, or Lance Armstrong, who overcame cancer and won the Tour de France seven times. Mahatma Gandhi observed that "Strength does not come from physical capacity. It comes from an indomitable will." Yet the will, like thinking, requires schooling. Starting with small, simple exercises and practicing them faithfully can help enormously to strengthen one's resolve. Having practiced daily, when a firm resolve is required later we can be surprised at how deep the reservoir has become.

Cultivating Equanimity

Early on a Sunday morning ten years ago the phone rang, I picked it up, and, between sobs, a friend struggled to tell me that her teenage daughter had died the previous night. As she was biking home with her stepfather, filled with exuberance and life, her bike had skidded and overturned. Her head had struck the curb and she had died instantly. She had gone to elementary school with one of my sons, and had been an especially dear friend. She had played soccer and cello with our boys and their classmates. The call was a cry for help. Could I come and talk with her? What could she do? How could she go on? How could she help her daughter after death?

When I arrived at our friend's house we embraced and sat. In that moment it became clear to me that our profound, indeed infinite sadness needed by some means to be held within a quiet embrace. I struggled to be with our friend. As she wept I experienced her utter devastation as well as my own deep sorrow, and sought to hold both in a space of abiding calm. I felt that if I could somehow live with these two opposites, fully within the tragedy of the event and yet also finding my way to a still center, I could be truly helpful to her. Together, gradually and tentatively, we found a way to speak of her daughter's life and death and continued life in spirit. We spoke of her many friends who, like us, needed time to grieve. Together we imagined a vigil and memorial that could honor her daughter and carry us through the tragedy of her loss, and that could help to sustain our loving connection to her in the spirit.

Life's sorrows and joys surround us. They move us, sometimes gently and other times like an earthquake that steals the very ground of our existence from beneath us. In undertaking contemplative practice our feeling life becomes more and more sensitive. Our heart awakens to feelings we knew only fleetingly or not at all. And yet, if this enhanced life of feeling is not to overwhelm and incapacitate us, we need simultaneously to cultivate equanimity. If this seems paradoxical, it is. Through a schooling of our feeling life we are open to a much richer domain of experience. But if, as we hope, our feelings are ultimately to become cognitive, that is to say they become a means of contemplative *knowing*, then we need to experience our feelings with equanimity. Even when beset by the most difficult trials of life we should not abandon our inner center; we should seek peace in every tumult.

True artists know this secret, I am certain. Otherwise how could a great playwright, poet, or composer write or compose in a way that stirs us to our very depths? They must feel all that we feel and more; they must perceive the interplay of outer and inner completely. They know the meaning of silent tears, they feel the anguished wail of a bereaved mother, and sense the warm glow of timid love in a shy glance. And yet if they are to write beautifully, then every word and phrase must be weighed, every part of the whole judged constantly for its artistic character. Each moment the artist hovers between vulnerability and control, suffering and action, uncertainty and precision, despair and creation. If they are to live a sane life, then beneath and surrounding it all they must learn to trust. It establishes within them the ground-tone of peace. The third exercise is the discovery of this trust that grants deep peace.

In chapter one, I described the essential exercise for equanimity. Recall that in it we rehearse an emotion from the past. We imagine the situation that caused us to become angry, sad, jealous, etc. Through remembering the details we recreate the whole field of experience; we feel its "undertow." Instead of going along with the overpowering dynamic of the emotion, we seek out a higher vantage point from which to see and examine the feeling. We try to set aside the governing emotion. In doing so the blind force of anger, sadness, lust, or jealousy lessens. We begin to understand the source of our emotional overreaction, and how particular outer and inner circumstances triggered and then amplified the dynamic. Remember, we are not trying to "flatline" our emotions or cultivate psychic numbness. This would be dangerous, disconnecting us from the world and possibly generating a pathological state in which we become unaware of our own effect on others. Think rather of the poet writing of loss, passion, outrage, or jealousy. An artist overwhelmed by emotion cannot continue to imagine, or to compose the lines that allow others to share in his or her feeling. The great artist is sensitive, yet imperturbable; battered, yet centered. If we are blinded by our rage, sorrow, lust, or jealousy, we will be handicapped in our actions. Like the poet, we cannot know ourselves or others, nor can we compose our lives, if our emotions overwhelm us. Life should, in this sense, become a work of art.

Through regular contemplative exercise we can find a right relationship to feelings. So practice feeling, but do so with high intent. Brooding merely exploits old emotions, whereas a centered wakefulness in our feelings allows them to inform us concerning deep mysteries about ourselves. When we illuminate hatred, jealousy, and lust, we convert feelings into scouts that run out far before us, telling us about the world. Whether you are a teacher in front of your class, a parent sitting on the edge of your child's bed, or a physician listening to the concerns of your patient, your cultivated and transparent feelings allow you to delicately participate in the inner life of the other. You discover the reason for their confusion, you sense their longings, and you learn about their worries. In other words, you can come to know through refined feelings. In the New Testament we hear that "Unless you become as little children you shall not enter the kingdom of heaven." The innocent way a small child looks at another person—open, tender, trusting, and non-judgmental—this is the way we should come to see each other. It can be the goal of our practice.

In addition to empathetic knowing, the transformation of the feeling life brings healing. Obviously, if we can find deep peace, the benefit to us is clear, but that benefit can also extend far beyond us. If we succeed in some measure in establishing equanimity in our feeling, then we will find that the disappointments and challenges we meet can offer unexpected possibilities. In the language of the psychiatrist and scholar Robert Jay Lifton, when confronted with the tragedy of the Holocaust, Hiroshima, or 9/11 we can react with revenge, or we can pause, find equanimity, dispel fear and rage, and learn from the tragedy so that we can act out of insight, and even love. It is precisely in tragedy that we learn to see life's depths, if we can sustain equanimity even there. Rather than feel panic or fear at these difficulties, we can be drawn to the sorrow and even the horror of our world, and so become helpers and healers, whose eyes and hands are not paralyzed but rather are guided under all circumstances— even those that bring tears to our eyes—by a centered, compassionate attention to others. Is there any more humane response than this?

Great souls have learned this lesson well. They are able to carry not only their own trials but also the burden of those under their care. Moreover they do so with a grace and lightness that belies the fullness of their heavy hearts. Nelson Mandela, the Dalai Lama, and Aung Sang Suu Ki are beloved because they have discovered the secret of empathic knowing and equanimity when confronted with the suffering of their community. They feel the pain of others, they practice compassion— "suffering with"—but they are not incapacitated by it. Their hearts are like a great crucible capable of carrying the suffering of all in their care, and still giving out encouragement, forgiveness, and joy. If it seems like a paradox, it is. And it is exactly this paradox that we should practice in life.

Positivity

Our last considerations point beyond equanimity to another characteristic we should develop, one that has been called positivity or loving. In 1995 I was at Columbia University working with the Dalai Lama for the first time. The formal session was followed by a reception during which a reporter questioned the Dalai Lama concerning his views of the Chinese. The reporter pressed him for his personal opinion of those who had so savagely invaded Tibet, destroyed monasteries, killed monks and nuns, and still today imprison and often torture his followers. The Dalai Lama agreed that the loss of Tibetan autonomy was a great tragedy, and said he would do everything within his power to regain self-governance for his beloved people. The suffering of his kinsmen caused him pain, he said, and should be stopped. But instead of angrily denouncing the Chinese and calling for retaliation, the Dalai Lama described a contemplative exercise. When he pictured the suffering of his people at the hands of the Chinese, he explained, he also sought to see the Chinese soldiers as they saw themselves. They saw their work as one of liberating Tibetans from the tyranny of a religious despot; they were freeing the Tibetans who in their ignorance believed in a god-king, His Holiness the Dalai Lama. In this way many of the soldiers had a high motive and were not to be viewed as evil, even though their actions were violent and hateful. Instead of outrage, the reporter got a lesson in seeing the good in one's tormentor.

The Dalai Lama sought to see something positive in those who persecuted him and his people. In every situation, no matter how dire, there is something worthy of the human being. Can we find it and then attend to it instead of the negative alone? This does not mean we should call good bad and bad good. We see with clear and steady eyes the injustices being done and may act to oppose them, but the unjust act does not blind us to the hidden good within each and every person. We hold up the noble dimension within the adversary and attempt to work with it. It is a faithfulness to the highest within each of us.

Most of us do not have to confront the responsibility shouldered by a world leader who must advocate for the fair treatment of millions of individuals. But we all experience injustice, unkindness, and neglect. How do we respond to such behavior and to those who perpetrate it?

We can be drawn into the spiral undertow of resentment and anger or we can work to see, even in them, the good. It is a practice of faithfulness to their humanity. Rudolf Steiner gave a practice for faithfulness that speaks to this worthy goal. He suggested the following exercise:

> Create for yourself a new, indomitable perception of faithfulness. What is usually called faithfulness passes so quickly. Let this be your faithfulness. You will experience moments—fleeting moments— with the other person. The human being will appear to you then as if filled, irradiated with the archetype of his or her spirit. And then there may be—indeed, will be—other moments, long periods of time when human beings are darkened. But you will learn to say to yourself at such times: "The spirit makes me strong. I remember the archetype. I saw it once. No illusion, no deception shall rob me of it." Always struggle for the image that you saw. This struggle is faith-fulness. Striving for faithfulness in this way, we shall be close to one another, as if endowed with the protective power of angels.[57]

When Nelson Mandela left prison after over twenty years of incar-ceration, he did not seek revenge against those who imprisoned him. The white minority was to have the same opportunity for participation in government, the same rights to own land and to be secure as the previously oppressed majority of black South Africans. In this Mandela turned his back on ethnic strife and Black Nationalism to affirm the truly human in everyone. He kept faith in the white as well as the black people of South Africa. He sought to see the highest within those who oppressed him, he led his government to pass laws of inclusion and not retribution, and together with Desmond Tutu he sought "truth and rec-onciliation" through a process of confession and forgiveness. In his inau-gural address Mandela affirmed his vision with the words,

> The time for the healing of the wounds has come. The moment to bridge the chasms that divide us has come. The time to build is upon

---

57. Rudolf Steiner, *Sprueche, Dichtungen, Mantren, Ergaenzungsband*, GA40a (Dornach, Switzerland: Rudolf Steiner Verlag, 2000), p. 286.

us..., we enter into a covenant that we shall build the society in which all South Africans, both black and white, will be able to walk tall, without any fear in their hearts, assured of their inalienable right to human dignity—a rainbow nation at peace with itself and the world.

Have not all great teachers said the same? Jesus said to his disciples, "But I say to you that hear, Love your enemies, do good to those who hate you.... If you love those who love you, what credit is that to you? For even sinners love those who love them.... But love your enemies, and do good, and lend, expecting nothing in return."[58] If we are to practice loving, then we must learn to see what is worthy of love within friends, strangers, and even enemies.

During your meditation, place before you someone with whom you have difficulties. Consider the problematic aspects of the relationship first, but then seek to move beyond them. Like the Dalai Lama, seek a higher motive beneath the surface behavior that offends you. Look for the positive, for the good. It may be difficult, but in the end you will inevitable find this aspect in those who seem to oppose you. Hold it, practice faithfulness to this high feature of their nature, and wish them peace, health, and joy in life. Practice loving kindness toward them in your meditation.[59]

Openness

In 1905 the patent clerk Albert Einstein published three papers that revolutionized physics. Together they did more to transform the way physicists look at the physical world than the papers of any scientist since Newton. How did Einstein do it? Two factors were paramount in making his achievement possible. First, he possessed a remarkably original genius and capacity for concentration. From his friends we have the picture of him writing his paper on special relativity while pushing a pram back and forth in his small apartment. He had strengthened his attention to the point where he could concentrate on a problem for months at time. However,

---

58. Luke 6:32 –35.
59. Buddhist practitioners will recognize the "loving-kindness" meditation or *Metta Bhavana* in what I have described. I will return to this meditation.

I believe that the decisive factor was Einstein's stunning openness to new ideas concerning the very notions of space and time. He had inherited the conventional notions of space and time that had organized all our human experience since time immemorial. For example, we say that objects *have* a length. Processes *have* a duration in time. That is, the things of the world possess spatial and temporal attributes. Sure, perspective can play tricks on us, but the object itself has a length. Look at a ruler end-on and it doesn't look at if it is twelve inches long. Correcting for such visual deceptions, we know that the ruler "in itself" is a foot long. However, according to Einstein's theory of relativity, for two observers in relative motion the length of the ruler will not be a foot or any other set amount. Instead the length will depend on the relative speed of the observers! Since Einstein declared that no reference frame is privileged over any other, no measured length is privileged over any other. That is, the differing lengths associated with different reference frames all have equal standing.

All of physics has changed in the wake of Einstein's special and general theories of relativity. We needn't change our day-to-day view of things, because the change in space and time is only noted at very high speeds, but they are real enough, for example, when engineering particle accelerators. I could repeat the same story for every scientific discovery, be it Copernicus's heliocentric solar system, Galileo's law of inertia, or wave-particle duality in quantum mechanics. The greatest barrier to their discovery and acceptance was the closed-mindedness of the scientists and intellectual community of the time. It is often remarked that powerful new theories rarely convince the old guard, but find general acceptance only after it has died off. The custodians of our intellectual culture see themselves as the conservators of a time-honored tradition, and this mental attitude works against open-mindedness. But openness to the new and unexpected is exactly what is required of the meditant as well as the creative scientist or artist.

Historians and philosophers of science have pointed out that we see the world in terms of our theories.[60] Concepts are much more than

---

60. Thomas Kuhn, *The Structure of Scientific Revolutions*, 3rd ed. (Chicago: University of Chicago Press, 1996); Owen Barfield, *Saving the Appearances* (Wesleyan, CT: Wesleyan University Press, 1988).

simple designators; they form the very structures by which we perceive the world. As Einstein once wrote, "It seems that the human mind has first to construct forms independently before we can find them in things."[61] Consciousness itself is shaped by our ingrained habits of thought. They form the ruts in which our perceptual system runs. "Objects *have* length!" That rut was and remains very deep because it is reinforced through daily experience. We maneuver our car through the world based on this honorable principle. If we could drive at near the speed of light, however, we could slip through traffic with very different dimensions. If you are having a difficult time imaging this fact, then you have bumped into the high walls of a rut in consciousness.

In order to overcome habits of perception you first must become aware of them, and then work to change them by entertaining alternatives. There are many aids to doing this. Visual illusions are one way. Consider the image below, called Fraser's spiral.

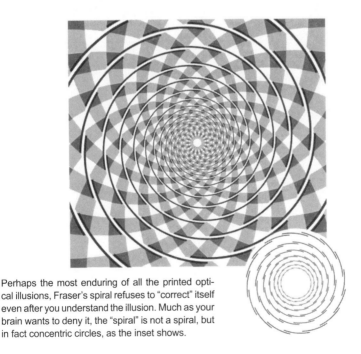

Perhaps the most enduring of all the printed optical illusions, Fraser's spiral refuses to "correct" itself even after you understand the illusion. Much as your brain wants to deny it, the "spiral" is not a spiral, but in fact concentric circles, as the inset shows.

61. Quoted in Arthur Zajonc, *Catching the Light* (New York: Oxford University Press, 1993), p. 253.

For most people, no matter how you look at it, the image is that of a spiral. However, if you trace one of the spirals you discover that you end up where you started. That is, the figure is really a set of concentric circles. Yet no matter how hard you try to see the pattern as concentric circles, it appears as a spiral. When circles are placed against a particular background, you are predisposed to see them as spirals. Strip away the background, as in the lower right of the figure, and it is instantly obvious that the figure is composed of circles. Our judgment is always contextual. We see holistically, judging the parts in relation to the whole. Even the absence of a background *is* a particular background. With this in mind we can understand Goethe when he declared that there was no such thing as an optical illusion and that "optical illusion is optical truth."[62]

Other habits are less well-ingrained. Look at the second image.

"I'm turning into my mother."

---

62. Quoted in Rudolf Magnus, *Goethe as Scientist*, trans. Heinz Norden (New York: Schuman, 1949).

The figure on the left of this New Yorker cartoon is unambiguously a young woman.[63] To the right, however, is a figure that can be seen as either an old or a young woman. Most likely one of the two alternatives shows itself immediately while the other is more difficult to find. Which is easier for you? This reflects your particular habit of mind. In this case you can "change your mind" relatively easily and train it to see the other figure. If you saw only the young woman, look at her chin and change it to a large nose with a wart. The young woman's necklace becomes the mouth of the old woman. Shift back and forth a few times. What is changing? Certainly not the figures themselves, but your interpretation of them. Some structures of consciousness are powerful and recalcitrant. Changing them may take a lifetime. Those who are, in effect, mental dinosaurs simply need to die off before a new way of seeing and knowing can establish itself. Other structures are easily modified. Einstein seemed capable of stunning changes in his mental structures, sacrificing space and time for a higher aesthetic beauty, namely the invariance of the laws of physics themselves. He gave up the fabric of conventional consciousness, not for chaos, but for something he perceived as a higher truth and deeper understanding of reality. As a final teaser, I leave the reader with an illusion entitled "Turning the Tables" that the cognitive psychologist Roger Shepard invented and made famous. I think it is particularly pertinent to our discussion of Einstein since the two tables appear to be of different lengths when, in fact, they are identical, differing only in orientation. Try to convince yourself of this.

---

63. Paul North, *The New Yorker*, August 28, 2006.

The closed-mindedness I have described so far is relatively benign. Simple visual illusions help us to discover the tacit mental structures that underpin perception by alerting us to the unconscious interpretations we make all the time. Such instantaneous judgment is essential to human survival and our normal functioning, but it can also blind us to the new, and to our prejudices. The history and philosophy of science inform us concerning the difficulties associated with advancing new and unfamiliar theories. My book *Catching the Light* can be read as concerned with exactly this, returning again and again to the changes that occur in the human mind as we seek to understand our place in the universe. Giordano Bruno burned at the stake for maintaining that the Sun was at the center of the solar system, and many thousands died at the hand of the Inquisition for their heretical beliefs; the battle over ideas simultaneously reveals our deep and usually unexamined biases.

The Holocaust and ethnic cleansing are obvious examples of prejudice's insane implications. We normally ascribe such behavior to others who are ignorant and emotional. Yet even science can be caught in the mire of bigotry. For example, in his study of the Nazi doctors Robert Jay Lifton demonstrated how science was calmly and systematically used to "prove" that gypsies, Jews, and others were vermin and must therefore be exterminated to safeguard human civilization.[64] Efficient technical means were devised to execute the millions of human pests. We "see" others who are unlike us as threatening, repulsive, or demonic. The catastrophes of ethnic conflict are only the extension of a myopia that sees the world from one vantage point and can only judge the world against one background, our own. Considered in this way, true openness is one of the most important intellectual and moral accomplishments to which we can aspire. In the realm of ideas it is required for discovery, but in the conduct of human affairs it is essential to our very humanity.

By incorporating a practice of openness into our daily meditation we prepare both for an outer life of engaged interest and for an inner life open to the unexpected and unfamiliar. As in other exercises we seek out occasions in our life that evidence lack of openness; we discover our

---

64. Robert Jay Lifton, *The Nazi Doctors* (New York: Basic Books, 1986).

closed-mindedness and prejudices. Instances should be found in the two realms I have described: prejudices concerning ideas and other human beings. I recently encountered an example of the former when a student approached me and asked what I thought of the new discovery that distant galaxies were accelerating away from us. Like most physicists I am approached by plenty of people with crackpot ideas, and everything I "knew" about cosmology said his claim was wrong. Distant galaxies were slowing down, not speeding up! I told the student that he must be mistaken. The next day I read about the startling discovery for myself and, after examining the astronomical evidence, had to agree that it indeed seemed to support my student's position. The data required an entire rethinking of relativistic cosmology, but sometimes that is the way scientific progress occurs. Being wrong can be thrilling! Once we discover our error, an entirely new way of seeing emerges; an unanticipated realm opens up before us. Our prejudices hide many wonderful truths about the universe and about our fellow human beings. If we can get past the closed doors of categorization, the worlds of those unlike us can become our world, and the greater the difference, the greater the enrichment.

As part of a class at Amherst College my colleague Joel Upon and I have taken students to a Camphill community for mentally handicapped adults.[65] Amherst students are some of the most capable and privileged young people in the nation. Most have only been around others who are like themselves. As part of our class for one day they enter a small village of two hundred inhabitants where half are mentally challenged, in many cases profoundly so. On the bus to Camphill, our students became quite nervous. Autism, Down syndrome, and spastic are terms whose definitions they could recite but whose meaning they had never experienced. They were full of expectations, misgivings, and longing, all at the same time. We were about to enter a territory they had never visited and will never forget.

As the big silver bus slowly wound along a dirt road to the Camphill community entrance, the tension built. The bus stopped, and from out

---

65. Camphill communities are to be found throughout the world. They work with mentally handicapped children and adults in a community setting. See www.camphill.org.

of nowhere thirty of the "villagers" streamed toward the bus. The arrival of so many visitors on such a grand bus was a real occasion at Camphill. They called out to Joel and me, whom they had come to know over the years. As we stepped out of the bus, our students lingered behind us. Joel and I were immediately caught up in a sea of warm embraces and rapid questions from several of the handicapped villagers. One by one our students tentatively descended the bus's stairs and were suddenly drawn into the forcefield of natural affection radiated by the villagers. A few minutes later they were sitting on the ground or standing in small circles, exchanging names, birthdays, and accounts of the small events of the past week.

Throughout the day our students would eat with these villagers in their homes and work with them in their craft shops, in the farmyard, and around the estate. We gathered in the evening for a final session with a leader of the community and with two of the villagers. We asked our last questions about their life and work in the community, and more often than not the villagers themselves answered them with a purity of feeling that spoke to the heart. On the bus ride back the air was animated with student conversations. "Why can't Amherst College be more like Camphill? Why can't it be more welcoming, warmer, more real?" Good questions. Why hadn't others thought to ask these questions? Through their experience at Camphill, our students learned about something they were lacking. They had arrived complete, with every advantage over those they visited, but to their credit they left with a sense of their impoverishment. They were open, as youth can easily be, to an unexpected teaching. Everyday we can learn to see our lacks, our limitations, and that is something of great significance.

To begin this practice, take an inventory of your prejudices. We each have a part of life we are reluctant to think about or explore, places we won't go, people we feel uncomfortable around. Who are they? We meet ideas that seem strange and perhaps even alarming to us. What ideas are they? Without accepting them outright, can we entertain the ideas of others? With a little practice we can greet the stranger, make eye contact with the homeless, have a heartfelt conversation with someone of a different faith or race. Like my students, we can learn to step out of the bus open to the unknown and initially unsettling encounter. When I was twenty-one I worked at a summer program for multiply-handicapped

Hispanic children on Chicago's Southside. I arrived for my job interview and was shown around by the director of the center. As we entered the first classroom, a disfigured, spastic girl of about fourteen stumbled toward me, her twisted teeth in a contorted smile, her arms outstretched to embrace me. It took all the courage I could muster to open my arms to her in return. We became friends that summer. Openness doesn't happen on its own; we need to practice it. We can practice it inwardly by calling up a difficult situation or person in our meditation and cultivating openness toward him or her. Whereas in the positivity exercise we sought the good in everyone, here we practice opening ourselves to that goodness. We trust that if we make ourselves available, then through such an encounter we will change for the better. This should also make clear that I am not suggesting that we open ourselves to the many destructive forces in our world. In every circumstance we find the beautiful and the positive. For this reason cultivation of a sense for the positive precedes the practice of openness. When we open ourselves, we do so to that which can nourish us. As with other exercises, having practiced openness in our meditation we are better prepared for openness in daily life.

Balance and Birth

I have described five practices that are intended as comprehensive care for the inner life. Through the first practice our distracted jumble of thoughts gradually becomes steady and reliable. By means of the second our many half-hearted intentions make way for firm resolves that endure and lead to real fruits. The tumult of our emotional life eases as we practice the third, and in place of turmoil a warm, lucid light of sensitive awareness connects us with the infinite subtlety of both the inner and outer worlds. With our feelings under our control, we train ourselves to avoid automatic reactions and seek the good in the other via the fourth practice of positivity. Finally, having discovered the good we can open ourselves to life with deep trust in the consequences. These five practices can circulate within us as a nourishing stream, harmonizing and balancing our contemplative life. They are profoundly hygienic and can be practiced over a lifetime. Patience is part of the practice, but we can rest assured that gradually the mud will settle and the water will become clear.

Rudolf Steiner recommends adding one practice each month so that by the fifth month all five are being practiced for a few minutes each day. During the sixth month one orchestrates all five, giving emphasis to those that are more needed. We know ourselves well enough to know whether our thoughts have become disobedient or our feelings have been captured by an emotion. The principle behind Steiner's suggestion is that self-knowledge and regularity will create all-important inner health. This becomes increasingly significant as we deepen our spiritual life. Under most circumstances we are unconsciously carried by conventional culture and civilization. Once we take up a serious meditative practice we gradually become liberated from convention and the social supports common to ordinary life. Original insights and perceptions arise, and with them new demands are placed on us. The mind or, to use the traditional term, the soul must be a fit vessel for the dawn of a full spiritual life. The five practices insure exactly this. They bring deep peace and equanimity, a steadiness to the light of attention, a generosity and a gentle firmness in all we undertake. These are obviously of universal benefit, but they are especially valuable for further meditative work.

The fifth-century Buddhist monk Buddhaghosa distinguished between two levels of accomplishment in meditation. Using a metaphor I appreciate, first he likens the meditant to a small child who is learning to walk. The child holds on to nearby objects or may need the helping hand of another person. One or two steps are all the child manages before falling down, but each step is accompanied by joy. Gradually, with renewed effort, walking becomes completely natural. One walks without concern until the goal is attained. The second stage of meditative accomplishment is like the latter form of walking. For quite some time we may struggle to take even a few steps in meditation without falling down. But occasionally, and then more regularly, our meditative awareness changes character, becoming fluid and graceful.

In this experience we recognize that we are caught up in processes and a presence that are beyond us. We sense that our mundane concerns have been set aside for a time and we participate in a larger and universal dimension of existence. This moment is variously described, but it can be experienced as an awakening, a kind of birth into a higher domain of experience, or the emergence of a higher aspect of the Self. It is a significant shift because this state of consciousness will become the surest basis for subsequent meditative work. From it one can work most effectively with mantra, verses, image meditation, and the like. It is from this stage of development that the great spiritual teachers taught. When reading sacred literature we sense that little or nothing of the mundane self is speaking. Instead the great, silent Self is giving voice to truths that transcend ordinary time and space. This voice speaks with an authenticity and depth that spans continents and centuries. Each of us in some measure can tap the source that fed the great teachers of humanity. Each of us can participate in the Self that is also the no-self, which can only be known after we have discovered the poverty and delusion of the conventional self. The mystery of this birth will occupy us repeatedly through the book. Call it Logos-consciousness, Buddha-nature, or Merton's silent self; each captures an aspect of that which ultimately defies representation or description. We find ourselves caught up in a presence that is far beyond us yet feels like our true nature.

In the face of such an experience we rightly feel and practice gratitude: thankfulness for each of the small successes, and even for the failures that teach us so much along the way. And finally, we know that what is given to us is really given through us to all of creation. We naturally release whatever gifts we have received and pray that they will benefit all beings everywhere.

Beyond Bliss

Before turning to the full range of meditative exercises that build on the practices described above, I must turn once again to the deeper motivation that animates the contemplative life. The personal benefits of such exercises as the above are many and invaluable, yet I think that the focus on benefits is too limited. Do we love and raise our children because they will take care of us in our old age? No, we do so out of love for them and their infinite potential, out of the joy we wish them in life and our hope that they may serve the entire world. Likewise, while one's initial motivation may be to seek help in handling a personal crisis or chronic physical pain, the long view of contemplative practice approaches the undertaking differently.

I have long been attracted to the line by Einstein, "I have never looked upon ease and happiness as ends in themselves. This ethical basis I call the ideal of the pigsty." Happiness is really not the goal of life. Einstein's life was not a commitment to happiness but a long commitment to inquiry. Goethe's Faust seals his bargain with the devil Mephistopheles promising to go with him if he, Faust, would ever say to the passing moment, "Tarry, thou art so fair!" In other words, Goethe saw striving, not bliss, as the central core of our humanity. Citing Augustine, Thomas Merton described human development as proceeding not in steps but via a sequence of "yearnings."[66] Its goal is the attainment of an inner paradise, which "is simply the self no longer clothed with an ego." This is Merton's language for the birth of the silent or selfless Self of which I have written.

It would be a misunderstanding and oversimplification of Buddhism's Four Noble Truths concerning the sources and relief of suffering to say that the goal of spiritual development is happiness or bliss. Within Christian theology it would be nonsense to ask whether Christ sought happiness on the cross. The life of Christ is meaningless without his passion and sacrificial death whereby he sought to relieve humanity from the "burden of sin." His life and the countless lives of those who have imitated him have been directed toward suffering, not away from it. Of course, I am not advocating suffering, but it is intrinsic to a life rightly lived. Struggle and suffering are inevitably associated with aspiration and compassionate concern. After all, compassion literally means "to suffer with." These considerations suggest another motivation for contemplative practice than the relief from personal suffering. It suggests that in meditation we turn our attention beyond ourselves, toward others and the world.

During a tea break between dialogue sessions in the Dalai Lama's residence in Dharamsala, India, the Dalai Lama and I shifted our discussion from the new physics and Buddhist philosophy to more personal matters. We were a small group, and he and I were seated just across from each other when I asked him, did he still have contact with the monks in

---

66. Thomas Merton, "Learning to Live," *Love and Living*, ed. Naomi Burton Stone and Brother Patrick Hart (New York: Harcourt Brace & Co., 1985), p. 8.

Tibet, and how were they faring? He obviously heard me but remained silent, looking straight ahead. After a long pause, my Buddhist friend Alan Wallace leaned over and said, "This subject is simply too difficult to speak of." I then realized what it meant to carry inwardly the suffering of so many, and understood also that the greatness of individuals like Nelson Mandela and Rigoberta Menchu Tum lay not only in their struggle for freedom, but much more in their ability to carry the injustices and the horrible suffering of an entire people. And, most importantly, for such individuals this suffering does not convert into the poisons of hatred and revenge. On the contrary, such individuals continually seek reconciliation and truth. The exercises concerned with inner hygiene strengthen us that we also may sense and carry the yearnings and sufferings of others more fully.

In the closing pages of his autobiography Nelson Mandela described how he came gradually to feel that his own freedom was inextricably entangled with the freedom of all the others who were living under apartheid. Concerning his experience of interdependence, Nelson Mandela wrote: "I am no more virtuous or self-sacrificing than the next man, but I found that I could not even enjoy the poor and limited freedoms I was allowed when I knew my people were not free. Freedom is indivisible; the chains on any one of my people were the chains on all of them, the chains on all of my people were the chains on me."[67] Compassion is rooted in the experience of interdependence. My freedom is inseparable from your freedom. While we are not Mandela, and our circle of concern is more limited, we all know what he was describing. We are one human community that must find a way to live harmoniously with each other and with the other creatures and life forms of our planet. Interdependence reaches far beyond the human species. The struggle along the long road to freedom, as Mandela called it, was just that, a struggle filled with the deprivation of a quarter century in prison, but also with the dignity of the free spirit that can never be imprisoned.

---

67. Nelson Mandela, *The Long Walk to Freedom* (Boston: Little, Brown and Company, 1995), p. 624.

As Rilke stated, "almost everything serious is difficult, and everything is serious."[68] All important and good work requires effort. Yet many struggles are unnecessary; they can be cleared away in order that we can live more fully, more joyfully, and more compassionately. This certainly is an important aspect of the contemplative path. Together with the significant personal benefit of contemplative practice, more profound and entirely selfless reasons exist for undertaking the meditative life.

---

68. Rainer Maria Rilke, *Rilke on Love and Other Difficulties*, trans. John J. L. Mood (New York: Norton, 1975), p. 40.

Chapter Four

Breathing Light: A Yoga of the Senses

The subjects for meditation are varied. One may, for example, choose to meditate on a passage from scripture, a sacred image, an experience drawn from nature, or a more complex inner situation. Each of these contents has its own character and force, but each can be fruitfully approached using the archetypal form of practice I introduced in chapter one as a breathing of attention. Recall that this form of practice involves a rhythmic movement between two poles: focused concentration and open awareness. Taken together, these two compose a type of "cognitive breathing" that makes use of the two primary varieties of attention. After reminding ourselves of the qualities, rhythm, and attitudes necessary for the different parts of this archetypal form of meditation, we will move to specific practices.

Cognitive Breathing

The first phase of cognitive breathing asks us to use our strengthened attention, concentrating on a specific content. We place the object of concentration—be it a word, image, sound, or object—before us in the left side of the lemniscate (the figure-eight of chapter one) and strive to concentrate on it with "single-pointed attention." We bring our entire attention to the object, noting its features carefully and fully. After some minutes, we release our attention from the object, and, moving to the right side of the lemniscate, we open our awareness wide. Inner silence and non-focal awareness are sustained. The rhythmic movement between focused concentration and open awareness comprises the archetypal form of meditation I will call cognitive breathing. I make use of this term because of the breath-like, rhythmic movement between concentration and open awareness. Instead of attending to the in- and out-breath, the meditant attends in two distinct ways to a word, image, or situation. The first phase of concentration is familiar to us, but we need to consider the second phase of open awareness more fully.

In the posthumous collection of her writings *Gravity and Grace*, the French author and mystic Simone Weil wrote concerning the "void."[69] Her words are remarkably helpful in gaining a sense for the experience of open awareness and what can flow into it. She contrasts the movements of the natural world, which are conditioned by physical laws such as gravity, with the characteristics of grace. The soul, like the stone, usually conforms to outer laws; it reacts habitually or conventionally, and our moods are driven by outer events or interior preoccupations. Weil describes grace as a liberation from these constraints: "All the *natural* movements of the soul are controlled by laws analogous to those of physical gravity. Grace is the only exception."[70] One can say that the practice of open awareness is an attention to grace, should it appear. Simone Weil knows that grace does not appear on demand. By definition this is impossible. But one can attend to grace. The precondition for grace is "empty space," or, in Weil's language, the void. "Grace fills empty spaces but it can only enter where there is a void to receive it, and it is grace itself which makes this void." The rhythmic movement between concentration and open awareness is designed to provide time and intention for grace to create and then enter the void. If we are fortunate, the gravity-like laws that normally constrain our soul's experience are momentarily suspended, the void opens out, grace enters, and another space of experience dawns. Simone Weil described such moments this way: "The human being only escapes from the laws of this world in lightning flashes. Instants when everything stands still, instants of contemplation, of pure intuition, of mental void, of acceptance of the moral void. It is through such instants that he or she is capable of the supernatural."

---

69. Simone Weil, *Gravity and Grace*, trans. Arthur Wills, reprint ed. (Nebraska: Bison Books, 1997).
70. Ibid., p. 45.

The Bell-Sound

Before going further, let us take up a four-part meditation on the sound of the bell, which presents us with a clear example of the cognitive breathing exercise used throughout this chapter. In brief, we first concentrate on the sense experience itself: the sound of the bell. Second, we attend closely to the memory of the sound. Once we are filled with the bell-sound, we let go and open our awareness as fully as possible while maintaining complete inner quiet. If grace appears, Simone Weil's "void" emerges within us and the final phase of the meditation can occur: "letting come." This phrase, used by the Chilean-born neuroscientist and contemplative Francisco Varela, beautifully describes the final stage of the meditation "when everything stands still" and the supernatural may come.

Choose a bell such as a chime or meditation bell with a long, resonant tone. Sound the bell and listen. Sound it again and attend to the temporal shape of the bell's tone, its abrupt call to concentration, its long, slowly fading reverberation. Strike it a third and final time so its complete nature is pressed deeply into your alert and listening mind, until it dies away into complete silence. Maintain your attention beyond the sound into the silence. You hear the memory of the bell-sound. The sound of the bell in memory can be heard as clearly as the real bell. Strike the bell in your mind. Your hands are still, but your mind can sound the bell within. Hear again the clear call and the resonant reverberation as it dies away to silence. Remember: where the reverberations end the meditative seeking begins. Once the sound has outwardly and inwardly fallen completely silent, shift your inner posture from directed to receptive, from focused concentration to open awareness, and hold the empty space without expectation. Make space in you for Simone Weil's void, and recall Lao-tzu's advice, "The Master does not seek fulfillment. Not seeking, not expecting, she is present, and can welcome all things."[71] Be present in a manner that can truly welcome all things equally. Have peace in your heart and openness in your mind, and discover the silent echo of the bell-sound.

---

71. Lao-tzu. *Tao Tè Ching*, verses 15 and 13.

Beyond Expectations

The mood we bring to open attention cannot be one of expectation or hope. Lao-tzu writes, "Hope is as hollow as fear." What does this mean? Lao-tzu answers, "Hope and fear are both phantoms that arise from thinking of the self." All our expecting is colored by our desires and by convention. In turning toward the void, we turn to that which is eternally new, unanticipated, and unique. How can we see a new face if we are only searching for familiar friends? In order to be able to welcome all things we must expect nothing, seek nothing, hope nothing. Only this inner stance can, as Steiner says, "...grant fulfillment now to wishes/ Whose wings have long been lamed by hope."[72] Instead, we patiently practice quiet, wakeful presence of mind.

Keats termed this a "negative capability," maintaining that literary geniuses like Shakespeare were uniquely "capable of being in uncertainties, mysteries, doubts, without any irritable reaching after fact and reason."[73] Or, in the words of the seventeenth-century poet and priest Angelus Silesius, "God is a pure no-thing/ concealed in now and here:/ the less you reach for him,/ the more he will appear." How strange it is that hope lames the wings of grace. Hope for spiritual awakening, desire it, and it will shyly slip away. In his *Four Quartets*, T. S. Eliot addresses his soul, calling it to heel, requiring that it wait without hope or desire.

> I said to my soul, be still, and wait without hope
> For hope would be hope for the wrong thing; wait without love
> For love would be love of the wrong thing; there is yet faith
> But the faith and the love and the hope are all in the waiting.
> Wait without thought, for you are not ready for thought:
> So the darkness shall be the light, and the stillness the dancing.[74]

---

72. Rudolf Steiner, *Calendar of the Soul*, trans. Ruth and Hans Pusch (Anthroposophic Press, 1982), verse for the twenty-eighth week.

73. John Keats, *The Complete Poetical Works and Letters of John Keats*, Cambridge edition (Boston: Houghton Mifflin, 1899), letter of December 22, 1817, to George and Thomas Keats, p. 277.

74. T. S. Eliot, "Four Quartets: East Coker III," *The Complete Poems and Plays* (New York: Harcourt, Brace and World, 1962), p. 126.

Without love and hope, only faith remains, and it is adequate for the waiting. Faithful, quiet, thought-free presence of mind is suited to light in the darkness, the dancing in the stillness, which is to say grace. Patience.

As should be evident by now, in meditation we seek to shift our consciousness away from the apparently firm material reality that is the constant feature of normal life and toward what at first appears to be nothing, or at best a reality far more elusive and ephemeral. Yet how secure, really, how enduring is material existence? Is not everything substantial prone to change and decay? Our own material existence is transitory like everything else. On what can we construct a truly enduring existence? When, after World War II, the Polish poet Leopold Staff walked among the ruins of his beloved country, the lines of this poem came to him.

I built on the sand
And it tumbled down.
I built on a rock
And it tumbled down.
Now when I build, I shall begin
With the smoke from the chimney.[75]

He titled the poem "Foundations." What we at first consider to be the secure foundations for a life may prove far more transient than we at first believe. And what may appear to be mere emptiness, perhaps briefly filled with a whiff of smoke or the scent of the rose, may become the basis for eternal life.

In cognitive breathing the concentration of the archer alternates with the attentive ear of the mother listening for her infant's call. The cultivation of silence is as significant as concentrated attention, perhaps even more so. In speaking with a student Rudolf Steiner said,

The most important, significant moments for our development in our exoteric life are those *after* the meditation, when we let absolute calm enter our soul in order to allow the content of the meditation

---

75. Leopold Staff, from *Postwar Polish Poetry*, ed. and trans. Czeslaw Milosz (New York: Bantam, Doubleday, Dell, 1965).

to work upon it. We should strive to extend these moments more and more; for through this "lifting ourselves" out of the circle of our everyday thought and feelings, through the "emptying itself" of our soul, we unite ourselves with a world from which comes towards us, pictures that we can compare with nothing our of our usual life.[76]

Remember also that the tempo of meditation is the same as that of artistic attention; it is the rhythm of poetry. Speed hides all subtlety, and reality is subtle. The model for this rhythm has always been the breath, but in our case the rhythm of breathing is to be translated to a more general rhythm of attention, a movement between the focal awareness and the soft, receptive gesture of open awareness. In all your practices remember to slow down; be led not by your thoughts but by your feelings, because feeling takes time.

The Language of Contemplative Experience

At this point in our journey we confront the thorny question of the language of contemplative experience. In writing about meditation I have, until now, attempted to avoid language that presupposes an explicit spiritual context for contemplative practice. The exercises described so far do not demand this of us. As we go further, however, we cannot avoid tackling the issue of language and the associated metaphysical considerations.

The mystical and spiritual traditions of all ages and cultures have developed comprehensive descriptive systems that allow them to communicate at least some aspects of meditative experience to those who share their cultures. Such languages have made extensive use of metaphor and a special vocabulary that contrasts the sensual and psychological with a transcendent domain of soul and spirit. While many modern practitioners of meditation know firsthand the exceptional states of consciousness induced by practice, they remain understandably uncertain or agnostic about their significance. Are meditative experiences entirely accounted for by changes in the brain's activity, or must we go beyond the material basis of consciousness

---

76. Rudolf Steiner, *Guidance in Esoteric Training*, (London: Rudolf Steiner Press, 1994), p. 155.

to account for them? For reasons I will explain shortly, I do not think we will ever get an unambiguous answer to this question. Is it possible to prove scientifically the existence of an immaterial spiritual reality? I think the answer is no; such proof will always elude us. But this need *not* imply that spirit (and God) do not exist. Absence of proof is not proof of absence.

Not surprisingly, this question has come up on various occasions in scientific discussions with the Dalai Lama. I distinctly recall one such occasion at the 2002 Mind and Life meeting on the nature of matter and life. A distinguished group of physicists and biologists had given a detailed materialistic account of the emergence of life and consciousness from matter and energy. I asked the Dalai Lama if this was consistent with his and Buddhism's view of reality. In his view and that of Tibetan Buddhism, he answered, there are two kinds of mind, one of which is constrained and limited by the brain and body, and one of which is not. Therefore the evolutionary story told by the scientists concerning the emergence of consciousness is entirely plausible for the former body-based mind, but the second type of mind that transcends the body is not susceptible to its limitations.

The scientists present at the meeting immediately asked for evidence for the immaterial dimension of mind. Among various facts, the Dalai Lama recounted stories of contemplatives in deep states of meditation and their reports of a so-called "clear light" state of consciousness, which is considered by Buddhists to be a form of awareness completely free of the body. How convincing are such personal reports? None of the scientists at the meeting changed their minds. Why not? By definition a contemplative experience is had by the practitioner and is inherently private; it is personal knowledge. Over a hundred years ago, William James recognized that mystical experiences have this distinctive character. Such experiences may be absolutely compelling to those who have them, but they lack that force for others.[77] Since God and spirit will not be bound by the usual rules of scientific investigation, they can always be plausibly denied.

The evidence that the mind and the nervous system are deeply connected is irrefutable, but we must proceed carefully. A simple analogy will suffice. You are reading this book, and there is a brain state corresponding

---

77. William James, *Varieties of Religious Experience*, lectures 16 and 17 on mysticism.

to that act. The book is not the brain state; the reality of the book is not called into question by the existence of neural correlates of the book in the brain. The report of a spiritual experience by a meditator will also necessarily entail a brain state. Like the book, it may be that the experience reported points to another aspect of reality beyond the brain state. Neural events themselves are ambiguous as to their referents. The stimuli may be outside us or inside us. A crucial difference between the book and meditative experience is that the former is an experience that is shared by all sighted people, while the latter is subjective. We can all look at this book and confirm its existence, while my contemplative experience is mine alone. In this way we return to William James's observation that mystical experiences are compelling only to those who have them. Yet even in a spiritual view there may well be a good reason why the spirit is so elusive.

In Fyodor Dostoevsky's *Brothers Karamazov*, the Grand Inquisitor confronts the returned Christ and accuses him of unpardonable restraint. For the sake of freedom, the Inquisitor declares, God has abandoned humanity to uncertainty, an uncertainty that he and the Church have, out of compassion, taken from them. God may want to be loved freely, but the burden of freedom is something people hasten to give away. It is simply too much for them, and its imposition on humanity has only been the cause of suffering. Refusing to give humanity incontrovertible proof of the existence of the divine is criminal, he insists.

Unlike the Inquisitor, I value the ambiguity in which we are left precisely because it does preserve our freedom in this existentially important domain of life. James was right; ultimately only personal experience will be the deciding factor. Meditation will have to be its own proof at every stage. Does it bring personal benefit? We will need to find out for ourselves no matter how many people say so. Likewise, the spiritual import of contemplative experience, when carefully developed and deepened, will be its own demonstration.

This can lead to a phenomenological stance that accepts the experiences as they arise but declines to interpret them. I see much that is sensible in this approach, as long as it is undertaken in good faith. In many instances little is to be gained by reaching beyond the experience for spiritual significance. The experience itself is meaningful and transformative. Yet I think that strict neutrality in this matter is neither viable nor helpful.

As meditative experience deepens, the language of the spiritual traditions is increasingly useful, and in the following pages I will make use of it where appropriate. If you remain agnostic about the issue, I ask your indulgence and good will. If you seek more detail concerning the spiritual context than I provide, I refer you to the extensive literature on the subject.[78]

Sense Meditation

The deepest words of the wise man teach us

the same as the whistle of the wind when it blows

or the sound of the water when it is flowing.[79]

— ANTONIO MACHADO

Thomas Merton, writing about the relation between solitude and love, echoed the sentiments of Antonio Machado, saying, "No words that were ever spoken can equal the sound of the wind in the pine trees."[80] Taking seriously the poets and contemplatives of our time, we can be confident in adopting nature as a subject for our meditation. She is as resourceful in her ability to teach as the sages who have taught us through the millennia. We can listen with benefit to the whistle of the wind in the pines and the sound of water flowing. Nature's purity helps to harmonize our emotions. In chapter two we discovered nature as a source worthy of wonder and reverence; now we can turn to her again for further contemplative purposes. By giving our attention to nature, we participate deeply in her ways and develop subtle faculties that can open up otherwise

78. Robert McDermott gives a comprehensive summary and anthology of Rudolf Steiner's and Sri Aurobindo's views in *The Essential Steiner* (San Francisco: Harper & Row, 1984), and in *The Essential Aurobindo* (Great Barrington, MA: Lindisfarne Press, 1987).

79. Antonio Machado, in *The Enlightened Heart*, ed. Stephen Mitchell (New York: Harper & Row, 1989), trans. Robert Bly, p. 129.

80. Thomas Merton, *Love and Living* (New York: Farrar, Straus, Giroux, 1979), p. 15.

invisible aspects of the world and ourselves. We learned how to practice cognitive breathing on the bell-sound. Turning now to the impressions offered to us by nature more generally, we can use the same method in order to take a step further in contemplative knowing.

The seventeenth-century Japanese poet Matsuo Bashō gave the following advice to his disciples:

> Go to the pine if you want to learn about the pine, or to the bamboo if you want to learn about the bamboo. And in doing so, you must let go of your subjective preoccupation with yourself. Otherwise you impose yourself on the object and don't learn. Your poetry arises by itself when you and the object have become one, when you have plunged deep enough into the object to see something like a hidden light glimmering there. However well phrased your poetry may be, if your feeling isn't natural—if you and the object are separate—then your poetry isn't true poetry, but merely your subjective counterfeit.[81]

In approaching nature as an object of contemplation, we can follow Bashō's advice to his poetry students. We must set aside all preoccupation with the self and turn our full attention to the pine or bamboo, entering into it completely. Then to our open mind it may show its "glimmering light" and thereby become word, that is, poetry.

Buddhaghosa recommends to the fifth-century monk that he make a bouquet composed entirely of yellow flowers and set them before him at arms length.[82] In this way the *kasina* (device) for yellow will become the object for meditation. The monk is to attend only to the yellow of the blossoms, allowing the green stems and all other particulars of the flowers to recede. The monk speaks the word, "Yellow! Yellow! Yellow!" He rejects all distractions, concentrating only on the color yellow. Having fully immersed himself in the yellow, he averts his gaze and allows the *nimita* or "afterimage" to arise. The *nimita* is not the complementary physiological afterimage that we all see when we saturate the retina with

---

81. Cited in Stephen Mitchell, *The Enlightened Heart,* Harper & Row, 1989), p. 155; and *A Zen Wave: Bashō's Haiku and Zen,* by Robert Aitken, (New York: Weatherhill, 1978).
82. Buddhaghosa, *Path of Purity* (London: Pali Text Society, 1975), pp. 143–204.

a color sensation. Buddhaghosa's description makes it clear that the meditant is seeking another kind of afterimage, one that is the interior correlate to the outer impression. Again and again the monk is to repeat the practice of concentrated attention on the yellow flowers before him, and then release. Into his open field of awareness there emerges the echo or afterglow of the sense impression. With sufficient practice the monk can stabilize the *nimita* or afterimage so fully that, if a passerby claps his hands next to his ear, the *nimita* of yellow remains undisturbed. If it wavers and disappears, then the monk knows that he must continue with this phase of the practice still further.

Speaking to an audience in Helsinki, Rudolf Steiner recommended a similar practice.[83] By enlivening our sense impressions, Steiner indicated, we can awaken to the living, spiritual dimensions of the Earth. Too often these impressions have become routinized and dead, and so are fit to perceive only the mechanical and material dimensions of our world. In order to expand our experience and understanding we need to deepen our sensual engagement with the world of color, sound, movement—indeed with all of sense existence. In this view the sense world is not to be abandoned when we take up a contemplative life, but rather our experience of it is to be transformed. The interior aspects of the outer world need to be uncovered and given our full attention.

Like Buddhaghosa, Steiner recommends a color exercise to his Helsinki listeners. We are to stand beneath the blue sky, and gaze into the azure color above us, uniting ourselves with it. We are to give the practice time, allowing the blue to fully permeate us to the point where the surrounding features on the horizon fade, and even the blue of the sky itself disappears. When we then turn aside, a distinct feeling arises in us. With each repetition a definite mood is more and more clearly established in our open awareness. Attempting to name such feelings is always a danger; we codify and so deaden the mercurial feeling alive in us. But if we had to put words to the experience, a feeling of devotion might be the best description.

Whether in the fifth century or the early twentieth century, the practice has the same key components. Both Buddhaghosa and Steiner are

---

83. Rudolf Steiner, *Spiritual Beings in the Heavenly Bodies and in the Kingdoms of Nature* CW 136 (Great Barrington, MA: SteinerBooks, 2009), Lecture 1.

advocating what I term a "yoga of the senses." First we are to concentrate on the color, becoming it and allowing it to become us. After identifying with the color as much as possible, we move to an open state of awareness in which an "afterimage" arises. Elsewhere Steiner describes the importance of this afterimage phase in these words: "The movement caused by the external impression has finished, and for most persons that is the end of the matter. This is, however, where the pupil must take his or her start...."[84] Exactly at this point, the point at which the outer effects of the sense impression disappear, we are to practice mindfulness of the void. We sustain the empty space, not seeking, not expecting, in order that we can welcome all things. With time and patience, grace does appear and the *nimita* arises like the Moon appearing from behind the clouds, as Buddhghosa would say. At first the experience is fleeting, emerging for a moment and quickly retreating. But with practice we come to trust the interior dimensions of the world in ways that are like our trust of the outer world. Our body moves through space confident that doorways will not slip sideways and the ground beneath us will not turn into water. Likewise, the language of the blue sky and yellow bouquet is trustworthy and steadfast. Our own emotions may be labile, but the interior gesture behind color is not. A single color will reveal many nuances that defy simple categorization, but color is not deceptive.

When faced with the difficult question of the aesthetic use of color, Goethe sought to create a science that would inform him not about color's mechanistic nature (wave or particle) but about its *sittliche* or "moral" aspect.[85] Goethe was working, I think, within the sensual stream of the contemplative traditions. He sought to move beyond opinion and prejudice in aesthetic and moral judgments, convinced that real insight in these matters was possible. Surrounded by Greek and Roman sculpture during his Italian journey, Goethe famously declared that the laws of artistic production were as certain and eternal as those of physical science. This flies in the face of contemporary postmodern deconstruction, which sees everything as social construct, but while the contemplative traditions

---

84. Rudolf Steiner, *Man in the Light of Occultism, Theosophy and Philosophy* (Blauvelt, NY: Garber Communications, 1989), Lecture 8, June 10, 1912.
85. Arthur Zajonc, *Catching the Light*, (New York: Oxford Univ. Press, 1993), Chapter 8.

are fully aware of the role of mind and context, they all reject the nihilist position implied by complete relativism.

For Goethe and those who think like him, the spiritual foundations of sense experience are secure; they provide a sure basis for self-transformation. The naturalist John Muir must surely have sensed the same full truth at the heart of nature when he wrote, "These blessed mountains are so compactly filled with God's beauty, no petty personal hope or experience has room to be." If we fill ourselves with the reality of the mountain or of the sky, the personal coloring we would add to the scene is squeezed out by the compact fullness of divine beauty. In this way, the purity of nature helps us to school our feeling. I have already written about the control of feelings as a preparation for meditation. In this phase that preparation is strengthened and our feelings are clarified and differentiated by sense-based exercises.

Both Buddhaghosa and Steiner consider other colors and sense experiences in their extensive treatment of sense meditations. To yellow, Buddhaghosa adds the *kasinas* for blue, red, and white. Steiner contrasts the color moods of the white snow field and green pasture with the mood of devotion discovered through the blue sky exercise. The meditator's palette takes on an interior reality, and the contrast of one color experience with a second makes the impact of a color's inner gesture all the more powerful. Having practiced the blue of the sky, switch your attention to the green of a grassy field or forest foliage. Feel the contrasting moods of these two colors. Or contemplate the white of the clouds so close to the blue sky and yet so different in their color tone. The experience is at once subtle and dramatic. The particular quality or presence of the blue is felt more strongly when juxtaposed with other colors.

Every painter knows how to emphasize one color by situating it next to another. The inner counterpart to this outer visual law is also real. We only truly come to know the character of one color through comparison with others. Think about it; if the world were only one color—monochromev—would we even perceive that color? Cognition comes only through comparison between diverse elements. Even when the eye is focused on a single object, it is actually moving quickly back and forth. In order to see, we must constantly compare. Stabilize an image on the retina, which can technically be done, and the eye stops seeing it. The requirement of comparison is a spiritual law as well as a physical one.

With this in mind one can appreciate how important it is to work with more than one color meditation. The variety allows us to map the inner soul space corresponding to the entire color space.

Neither Buddhaghosa nor Steiner ends the practice with color at this point. The generation of the first afterimage or *nimita* is followed by further exercises that use the afterimage itself as the object of meditation. Once the echo or afterimage has been stabilized sufficiently, it can be placed before our interior meditative eye, and the bouquet of flowers and blue sky are left behind. At each stage of the journey the slow, rhythmic interchange of focal concentration and open awareness is repeated. What has been the fruit of open awareness becomes the object of concentration. A second empty space is sustained, a new void opens, and a higher-level and purer afterimage presences itself. The journey leads to the archetype of yellow and blue, which has neither form nor the least trace of externality. Yellow loses its outer object nature and is experienced as a particular state of pure being. In the transition from sense experience to its interior counterpart, we realize the first step on the path toward contemplative knowing.

The exercises I have described for color can be applied to other sense experiences as well; for example to the elements of earth, water, air, and fire, or to sounds, plants, and animals. Indeed every feature of the sense world becomes an occasion for practice. All are further occasions for sense meditation, bringing ever greater detail and depth of experience to one's inner soul-scape.

The Elements

The nature of things is water;

the all is alive and is full of gods.

— THALES

The ancient Greek philosophers conceived of the universe as comprised of five substances. Four were the so-called elements of earth, water, air, and fire, which accounted for everything between the Earth and the

Moon. The fifth was the divine and immutable "quintessence" or ethereal substance out of which the perfect Sun and stars were made. Modern chemistry and physics organize 100-plus elements according to their properties and electron configurations. To the Greek mind everything around us could be understood as a combination of the four material primitives: earth, water, air, and fire. In Eastern thought, Buddhaghosa's ten *kasinas* include the four elements in addition to the four colors, light, and space. Many traditions, ranging from ancient Chinese alchemy to Rudolf Steiner's contemplative path, work with the qualities of the elements as an essential part of the meditative journey.

Bring your attention to a stone or a bowl of firm, dark earth. Select for yourself a sample of the earth and make it the object of your meditation. Consider its characteristics. If you have chosen the stone, feel its weight; observe its fixed shape, its unyielding surface, its self-contained quality. What are its colors: Is it warm or cool? What is its texture? Having entered deeply into the experience of the stone, turn aside or close your eyes and sustain the empty space of open awareness once again, silently. Most likely a memory of the stone will appear. You will see its shape and varied colors, and feel its surface again with your mind's eye. Intensify the memory image. Give yourself the time needed to fully re-envision the stone. Then continue by releasing the memory image completely in order to make room for the echo or afterimage of the stone. The difficult practice of silence, without expectation, but with presence of mind, begins. Sustain the empty, silent space. Repeat the exercise, turning rhythmically and slowly between concentration on the stone and open awareness. With time, a tentative feeling will emerge in the space held open. Allow it to take shape and reveal its subtle character. The specific character of this experience can vary widely, but it will have some sense-like character to it: color, warmth, movement, sound, a dark shape or gesture. Repeat the exercise until you can confidently sense these qualities inwardly associated with the stone. Then, as if the stone has left a trace behind, we are able to sense the lingering presence of the stone in the space before us, or perhaps within us—what we may think of as soul space. Allow the inner presence of the stone to remain where it is, but then, with your eyes open, pour yourself a shallow bowl of water.

Water now becomes your object of meditation. Observe it intently. Move the bowl slightly and notice the delicate movement of the water's surface. Notice how it conforms in shape to the vessel containing it. Observe that its surface is flat and parallel to the surface of the Earth— tip the glass and the water's surface stays parallel to the ground. Swirl your finger in the water; it is clear, cool, and wet. Observe how different it is from the stone: clear, compliant, mobile, wet, responsive.... Detail the many properties of water that you can perceive directly. Avoid textbook facts or associations, but rely on all your senses. Again, having concentrated on the water, turn aside or close your eyes and sustain the empty space of silent open awareness. If a memory arises, proceed as before. When the memory picture has been developed and explored fully, release it also. Allow the gesture or quality of water to arise fully in consciousness. Do not attempt to "see" something. Instead simply allow your open awareness full play. What does water "feel" like to you? Repeat the exercise until you are confident that you have found a deep feeling for the inner gesture of water.

Now juxtapose the felt qualities of stone and water in your interior space. You may need to attend for a moment or two to the neglected stone until its faded presence is re-enlivened within you. Appreciate the differences between the inner gestures of stone and water as they appear side by side. Since comparison can be a powerful experience and an important tool, give it time to develop. Be patient or repeat the exercise as often as necessary.

To earth and water we can now add air. Since it is all around us, we do not need to take it from the ground or pour it into a bowl. Air is present around us and inside us, but it is mostly unobserved until a breeze stirs and we feel the wind on our cheek, or see the fluttering of leaves on the trees, or the bending of a field of grass, or the shimmer of light in the dust as it blows through space. Then we notice the air. On a summer afternoon I stand outside and watch the wind, especially the leaves on the maple trees arrayed before me. Their leaves are still at first, but as the wind stirs they begin to sway and then to flutter, a sound of rustling may join the movement, and I imagine the vast, empty space around me full of leaves rustling in the wind. These leaves are invisible, but in my mind's eye they respond to the omnipresent movement of air. As when a crystal-clear stream of water distorts the creek-bottom, the wind fills space shimmering from the Earth's surface to the sky's limits. Even when the wind dies away, the air remains. As much as their motion, the stillness of the leaves reveals the air to me. Drenched with these impressions, I turn aside and sustain the open interior space into whose void the afterimage or soul gesture of air may emerge. Can I feel it, sense its shape and movement, its diaphanous quality? Repeat the exercise until, as before, you come to know the inner aspect of air. Now place this experience beside that of water and earth. Observe the differences. Do not think; simply observe. Stone is not water, water is not air. Each has its own nature. Sense them each and their differences.

Studied in this way, the elements and colors form an alphabet of inner experience. Like Plato's famous allegory of the cave in which the prisoners can only see shadows and surfaces, we have been misled into seeing only the external aspect of things. Meditation on sense objects shifts our attention to another aspect that is typically neglected. We break the chains of habitual consciousness and train our observation to sense the subtle soul gestures of everything around us. We are learning an interior language that will prove essential for our later stages of meditative practice and experience. Every sense experience becomes an occasion for deep engagement and the rise of its inner correlate. While performing these sense exercises you will likely notice that even before you turn aside, the afterimage dawns, laying its own special character over the familiar outer experience of the object, infusing it with an animating spirit. In my description of the exercise I have staged the different parts of the experience to make each clear. What I made sequential in time often appears almost simultaneously. I think that when John Muir repeatedly beheld the mountains, streams, and air of the wilderness, he saw in this twofold way, simultaneously perceiving the outer and inner realities around him and in him.

We are now in the mountains and they are in us, kindling enthusiasm, making every nerve quiver, filling every pore and cell of us. Our flesh-and-bone tabernacle seems transparent as glass to the beauty about us, as if truly an inseparable part of it, thrilling with the air and trees, streams and rocks, in the waves of the sun,—a part of all nature, neither old nor young, sick nor well, but immortal. Just now I can hardly conceive of any bodily condition dependent on food or breath any more than the ground or the sky. How glorious a conversion, so complete and wholesome it is.[86]

Muir is right: unlike our own interior, which is littered with TV commercials and untransformed desires, nature is wholesome. We can trust her as we cannot trust ourselves, and for this reason she offers a perfect basis for meditation. Starting with nature's colors, sounds, and substances provides a healthy means for the shaping of our spiritual nature. Nature never exploits, is never deceitful. Thus, as long as we remain wakeful before her, we can confidently take her mysteries into ourselves as templates for our new humanity.

Light

Earth, water, and air do not exhaust nature's bounty. Buddhaghosa included light and space in his list of the ten *kasinas* suitable for meditation. In turning away from the material world towards light, we find ourselves challenged to attend contemplatively to the insubstantial. We are constantly in light's presence but uncertain of its nature. Without it we cannot see, but we never see light itself. In this sense it is at once elusive and essential not only to sight but to life as well. Plants, animals and humans would wither away without its nourishing energy. I have explored the nature of light fully in *Catching the Light*; though here we are not interested in the physics or history of the concept of light, but rather a contemplative engagement with light itself.

The meditation on light is different from the one that encompassed the previous elements. Begin with light's absence. The experience of outer darkness prepares us for the dawn or the lighting of a candle. So too in meditation we must allow darkness its due. Sense the surrounding density and mystery of darkness prior to first light. In the dark all color and form disappears from view, and as we have no awareness of what is around us, we waver between extending ourselves into the surrounding dark and drawing ourselves back in. Then, if we ignite a match, light's

---

86. John Muir, *My First Summer in the Sierra* (Boston: Houghton Mifflin, 1911), Chapter 1, Part 2.

radiant power swiftly fills space from here to infinity, silently extending its reach forever. Remarkably, if light meets nothing substantial, then that illuminated space remains as black as the sky of the Moon (which, lacking an atmosphere, is never blue).

Through reflected light, distant objects like the Moon present themselves to us across space. The features of the landscape or even of the room you are sitting in are connected to you through light. We are placed into relationship through light. Feel these qualities of light as you observe the light phenomena around you. Sense not just the luminous objects themselves, but the light that is *between* you and everything you see. Appreciate the particulars of the relationship that light makes possible. Shift your attention increasingly away from the objects seen and toward that which works unseen between everything, gently and invisibly weaving disparate parts into a whole. Moreover, the brightness of light stimulates and uplifts us, while darkness draws us into silence that extends us into the unseen all around. Allow light to enliven you.

Close your eyes but cultivate the qualities of light in consciousness. Feel its weaving presence around you connecting you to all being, seen and unseen. Allow its uplifting power to raise you high. Light can be felt within as well as experienced without. You may or may not have an experience of brightness in your meditation on light; this is quite individual and is of no consequence. Everyone can sense the difference between the inner presence of light and the presence of darkness. Discover this difference for yourself as you live your way into light inwardly. When you are filled with light be silent, let go, and let come. Sit with the afterimage or soul gesture of light.

Through millennia light has been a token and symbol of the spirit, but also of overweening pride. Lucifer's name means "the bearer of light." Like Icarus, son of Daedalus, we must take care that our meditative flights do not carry us too close to the Sun. The force of light is both powerful and real. Through a deep identification with streaming light we can be carried very far in our meditation. Balancing levity with gravity, the architect and builder Daedalus knew the mystery of weight as well as light. He was mature in his flight, but young Icarus's enthusiasm overwhelmed his judgment. At every stage of the meditative journey we are called upon to practice good judgment, to sense how long and how far to go. If you sense that you have traveled too far in your meditative journey, remember Daedalus and reconnect yourself to the needs and duties of earthly life. Ground yourself inwardly by recalling the gravity of the tasks you carry, the love you have for friends and family. The "inner hygiene" practices with which we precede each session keep us grounded when light's glories threaten to overwhelm us. Meditative awareness needs to be supported by a calm and centered presence of mind. Patience, modesty, and common sense are antidotes to over-enthusiasm, vanity, and fantasy, providing much-needed balance in our practice.

From Light to Love

In addition to the four elements of earth, water, air, and fire, the Greeks spoke of a quintessence or "fifth essence." Corresponding to the elements of earth, water, and air that form the substantial part of our universe, we can imagine a set of quintessential correlates that together compose an ethereal realm. Each of the correlates can become the subject of contemplative attention. Light, for example, can be thought of as the quintessential correlate of air. We can proceed further to the quintessential correlate of water, which I will call love, and then on to the correlate of earth, which I will call life. Light is not the only invisible reality that weaves around us, informing and enlivening space. Our considerations of love as a process in nature will require much of us, but the rewards for entering into its kingdom, which is one of wise interconnectedness and transformation, are many.

The exercise on love in nature asks us to live into the processes and formative wisdom that are constantly unfolding about us. Take, for example, the cycle of water, which we can follow imaginatively. From darkening clouds, rain begins to fall, gathering in puddles and running down hillsides into creeks and rivers. From there we see it traveling to lake and sea, and under the bright rays of the Sun water is lifted to the sky again. Science can detail the process, but our intention is to participate in the cycle, living it. Nature's marvelous processes of transformation, occurring constantly in the physical world, are now invited into our mind and heart. We patiently and vividly live our way into cloud, rain, creek, and sea. In the language of cognitive breathing, we focus our attention upon a natural process or cycle, living our way into it exactly as we did the bell-sound. Enter into each phase of the cycle deeply, and then be silent and open. Move to open awareness without expectation.

If light establishes relationships, then into those relationships can flow a remarkable force: the genius of love. We might image love as a second light in the first: light in light. Nature is harmoniously constructed and ecological at every level, from the single cell with its thousands of processes to the planet's interwoven realms of minerals, plants, and animals. These reveal to us an intelligence that is at once dynamic, unitary, and loving. We can live into the processes of nature, becoming the cloud, the rain, the river and sea. We can move through cycles of day and night, of the seasons and stages of life. Mighty forces and wise laws rule the kingdoms of nature. Little by little we experience the harmony of those forces in the depths of our soul; we not only think them but live them.

We have learned how to become the cloud, rain, river and sea, going through all the transformations of water. Though what is of import is not the water but the change. Keep your attention not on the medium but on the transformation it undergoes. We become that which passes from the wind to the fluttering spring leaf, and on to the brittle autumn foliage; we enter into the manifold forces and loving wisdom that unfold around us. We are in them, and they are in us. Pythagoras spoke of the experience of the harmony of the spheres, of the experience of divine number in everything. Perhaps this is what he meant. Not dead mathematics but number in movement, permeated with warmth. This meditation deepens the experience of light. Light itself seems to carry in it a force that shapes and a wisdom that guides. As we live into light, we can go further to experience a wisdom that is also love in the light. We could call it formative wisdom, but I will call it love. Beyond ordinary *eros*, this love is a transformative genius that can infuse all relationships.

As for the light exercise so also here: maintain your inner balance during the course of meditation; be mindful of your own reach and when you have overextended. Even more than before, in this exercise we can feel carried far away toward the infinite and into the beautiful relationships that operate ceaselessly through the universe. At the close of the meditation, guide yourself back by recalling the full importance of all that awaits you here upon this good Earth. Be Daedalus (not Icarus) during your flight; you still have much good work to accomplish. This is, after all, the very reason you have taken up a meditative life, to be of greater service. Having lived the wisdom that works and breathes through the universe, we can bring so much more to human society. The journey home joins contemplative experience to the practical life: *vita contemplativa* to *vita activa*.

From Love to Life

The third stage of the meditation carries us to the final quintessential correlate, which I call life. Life is a third light, one I associate with meaning and purpose. If the nature of light is to create relationships, and that of love is to bring wisdom into those relationships, then in the final stage those relationships take on life. The quartz crystal, perfect and complete in itself, is nevertheless different from the flowering iris. The crystal is an image of light and wisdom, whereas the iris lives out its life before our eyes, sprouting, growing, flowering, withering, and decaying. The culmination of the three-part light meditation is to enter into the life and death of nature, to know its coming into being and its passing away. Through this phase we learn to be born with the sprouting corn and to die with the withering husks. The cycle of life is no longer a merely physical sequence but an unfolding interior drama of flourishing and failing, patterned on the endless reality of life and death in all realms: plant, animal, and human. Take into your meditative concentration the cycle of life, from birth and blossom to death and rebirth, as you see it unfolding around you. Practice cognitive breathing on this ceaseless process of becoming and passing away, ending with open silence, centered expansiveness.

The three lights can also be thought of in terms of sound. Light is like the pure monotone that establishes a connection between source and ear. Through the simplest sound I am aware of the presence of the other. But the tone can be formed or modulated into a cry. Through it I can recognize whether it is human or beast, bell or bird. This corresponds to the second light of formative wisdom, or what I called love. The third stage arises when sound is shaped into speech and magically we no longer hear mere sound or cry but meaning. Language informs and transforms sound so that it can carry thoughts and intentions. The third light, which I call life, likewise carries meaning and purpose. Purposeless growth is profligate and cancerous. The tree must give fruit, the seeds be formed.

Unrestrained life is as dangerous as dry death. The word gives sound coherence and direction. The third principle *life* should be thought of as carrying the remarkable force of the word within it also.

When meditating meaning-filled *life* we run the danger of personal annihilation because the power of the practice is so great. But, as described in Goethe's poem "Holy Longing," we can dare it. Humans are indeed like moths who hover around the candle flame, and who must find a way to pass safely the trial of fire, flying into the flame, dying in order to become. Goethe writes:

> The gleam of the silent candle fills you with a strange emotion. You remain a prisoner no longer in the shadowing darkness, and a new desire snatches you upwards to a higher union. No distance can weigh you down, you come flying, fascinated, and at last, lusting for the light, poor moth, you perish in the flame. And until you possess it, this commandment: Die and become! you will be but a dismal guest on the dark earth.[87]

If we have worked our way stepwise to the flame of dying and becoming, if we have felt reverence before nature and committed ourselves selflessly to service, then the death of the husk, which is to say our lower self, is nothing fearsome. We are certain to uncover the real self thereby.

Warmth: This Am I

> *Nature is an Aeolian harp—she is a musical instrument*
>
> *whose tones again are keys to higher strings in us.*
>
> — NOVALIS

The bridge between the elements and the three lights is warmth. From the standpoint of physics warmth is not a state of matter (solid, liquid, or

---

87. Goethe, *Selected Verse*, ed. David Luke (New York: Penguin Books, 1985), p. 240.

gas) but rather the agent of change. Heat ice and it becomes liquid water. Heat water and it becomes steam. Warmth disorganizes and dissolves rigid substance, opening it to change. The chemist heats her reagents to accelerate the chemical reaction. Fire causes change and is the agent for transformation on every level. Warmth permeates all substance to some extent making it hot or cold, which we measure through temperature. While warmth is not a "thing," it is in everything.

According to Greek myth, the element of fire was given to forgotten humanity by Prometheus and became our greatest boon. As Plato tells the story, at the dawn of creation all animals received a gift: the bear was given warm fur, the gazelle great speed, but the human was naked, weak, and unprotected. Prometheus stole fire from the gods and gave it to humanity as our distinctive gift. We warm ourselves by the fire and live. Yet the fire symbolizes the mind as well. Where the cat has fur, and the turtle its protective shell, the human possesses the fire of intelligence. It is our unique and defining possession. When meditating warmth we feel at home. We have the body, we aspire to the light, but we live in the warmth. Discover your warmth organism. Feel the warmth within you and around you. Are your limbs cool; is your heart warm? Close your eyes and rest in the peace and security of Prometheus's supporting gift to us. Practice on warmth, outside and inside.

Earth, water, air, and fire, light, love and life, these seven make up a graded meditative sequence that reaches from the solid earth to purposeful life. We have come to know each separately. Now it is time to weave them together, as they really are. Each of the seven can be experienced in two places: in the world and in us. Experiencing the parallel truths of outer and inner can become a way to share in the circuit of nature. All her elements and lights are within us. I use the meditation below to help cultivate in me a participation in nature's spiritual depths. With Arne Næss and the Native peoples of all continents, I am certain that our responsibility toward nature arises from our lived experience in her. Meditating our shared nature can go far in promoting that sense of responsibility.

This am I

Sitting quietly, feel your bodily nature.

I am the Earth.
[Imagine the mineral substances of the earth: soil, stone, and mountain. Feel these substances also in yourself. Silence.]
This am I.

I am the Waters.
[Imagine the rivers and seas, the mists and rain. Feel also the presence and flow of the waters in the body. Silence.]
This am I.

I am the Air.
[Imagine the blue sky through which the winds move, rustling leaves and grains. Feel how you take the air into yourself in breathing, how it flows through the body, spreading, enlivening. Silence.]
This am I.

I am the Warmth.
[A fire or the Sun warms the outer earth. In me too is living warmth, an inner fire. Feel it. Silence.]
This am I.

I am the Light.
[The light's presence brightens everything everywhere, making all things visible, bringing all into relationship. In me, too, is light. Feel it. Silence.]
This am I.

I am the forming wisdom of Love.
[In and through the light sounds the forming wisdom of love that is the harmony of the spheres. The harmony sounds in me also. Feel love's sound and its forming power. Silence.]
This am I.

I am the living Word.
[The sounding is no mere noise, but meaning, alive, Logos-born. Sense the Word in the word. Sense it in me. Feel the luminous, sounding,

wisdom-filled love that flows through world and self. Silence.]
This am I.

Earth, Water, Air, Warmth, Light, forming Love, and living Word.
All these are in the world. All these am I.
[*Silence.*]

Meditating in this way can help us form a true spiritual relationship
to the Earth, one that is a modern counterpart of what was and remains
a tradition within the Native American communities. Arne Næss placed
the experience of profound ecological interconnectedness at the heart of
his philosophy of "deep ecology" and recognized the spiritual foundations for ecological ethics. Satish Kumar called it "Reverence Ecology."[88]
As Schweitzer, Næss, Kumar, and so many others rightly acknowledge,
an ethics governing humanity's relationship to the Earth cannot be the
outcome of a rational cost-benefit analysis merely, but must be predicated
on a lived spiritual relationship to her.

From Stones to Stars

Although fourteen years his junior, Henry David Thoreau died before his
friend and mentor Ralph Waldo Emerson. Upon Thoreau's death, Emerson
insisted on a church service, although Thoreau never attended church, and
also upon delivering the eulogy himself. In his eulogy he expressed his
love, and also gave words to what he saw were Thoreau's special gifts. Yes,
Thoreau was a remarkable naturalist, pulling fox cubs out of their holes, hik-
ing through his beloved swamp, building boats for the New England rivers
and a cabin on Walden Pond. Yet for all this, he was so much more than
a frontiersman. "His robust common sense, armed with stout hands, keen
perceptions and strong will, cannot yet account for the superiority which
shone in his simple and hidden life," Emerson told his audience.[89] Emerson

---

88. Satish Kumar, *Resurgence Online*, "Learning from Nature," http://resurgence.gn.apc.
org/satish/kumar-nature.htm.
89. Ralph Waldo Emerson, "Eulogy for Henry David Thoreau," in *Walden and Civil
Disobedience*, ed. Owen Thomas (New York: Norton, 1966), p. 272.

recognized in Thoreau a special faculty of mind, one that allowed him to move beyond the literal to the figurative, to see in the facts of this world the aura of another. Emerson said to those gathered at the service, "I must add the cardinal fact, that there was an excellent wisdom in him, proper to a rare class of men, which showed him the material world as a means and symbol. This discovery, which sometimes yields to poets a certain casual and interrupted light, serving for the ornament of their writing, was in him an unsleeping insight." The Concord woods and waterways, which Thoreau loved as his true home, hid within them another landscape that spoke to him with equal force. Every natural fact was pregnant with the light of that other world. His task was to give expression to it. Emerson, who had known Thoreau since his graduation from Harvard College, recalled a conversation with Thoreau as a young man. "In his youth, he [Thoreau] said, one day, 'The other world is all my art; my pencils will draw no other; my jack-knife will cut nothing else; I do not use it as a means.' This was the muse and genius that ruled his opinions, conversation, studies, work and course of life." Thoreau's constant journeying along woodland paths and streams was his heart's response to the call of his muse and genius. Earth, water, air, and the morning light awakened him to a "poetic and divine life," until he became America's bard of nature. His *Walden* is one long song sung at the place where his two worlds flowed into one another.[90]

> Time is but the stream I go a-fishing in. I drink at it; but while I drink I see the sandy bottom and detect how shallow it is. Its thin current slides away, but eternity remains. I would drink deeper; fish in the sky, whose bottom is pebbly with stars.

In truth, Thoreau had no choice. He could do nothing else. While Emerson consulted his celestial spirits for inspiration, Thoreau consulted the stream, stones, and sky, seeing the river's pebbly bottom strewn with stars. When we meditate a sense-object, its thin, conventional nature "slides away," but its eternal nature remains behind. If we would drink

---

90. Henry David Thoreau, *Walden and Civil Disobedience*, p. 66.

deeper, if we would fish not only in the stream but also in the sky, then we must learn to whittle and draw the other world. Contemplating nature is learning to carve the contours of the unseen, and to draw the fluid forms of life.

Our true relationships in life are never to the material side of things. Reflect for a moment and you will recognize that you love your child or your garden or a poem because you have worked your way through its exteriority to an interior relationship with it. Of course the fragrance of lavender occurs via olfactory stimulation by a complex long-chain polymer, but we sense through matter to the soul of the world. Sense-based meditation furthers this process; it moves us from the scent through emptiness to the felt echo of the lavender's fragrance. By doing this our dependency on material sense impressions in thinking and consciousness generally is diminished. We enrich and clarify our life of feelings, and thereby create a landscape in us as rich, varied, and lucid as the sensual landscape outside us. Later, as material existence falls away, our work with the senses will prove invaluable. Because we have gained fluency in an inner language of soul, we are well prepared for the challenges of a dawning new reality that defies materialistic conception. Earth, water, and air really do drop away. As they fall we are supported in our awareness by their inner counterparts, and so, feeling secure instead of fearful, we can learn to know and to act in another world, a spiritual domain as well as a material one.

The senses offer us a wealth of impressions. Using the four elements and three lights (light, love, and life), we have begun the deepening of the sense world. Every touch, sound, and scent can be similarly deepened. The practice becomes for us a breathing in light, a yoga for the senses. Concerning these practices Steiner spoke about the "development of a breathing of the soul-spirit within the cognitive process through perception and thinking."[91] Perception and reflection become the systole and diastole of the mind. Rhythmically practiced, they comprise the archetype of cognitive breathing that shifts our awareness from stones to stars.

---

91. Rudolf Steiner, *Boundaries of Natural Science*, trans. Frederick Amrine and Konrad Oberhuber, October 3, 1920 (Spring Valley, NY: Anthroposophic Press, 1983), p. 121. Steiner gives great emphasis to sense-based meditations. See for example *How to Know Higher Worlds* (Great Barrington, MA: Anthroposophic Press, 1994), Chapter 2.

CHAPTER FIVE

Words, Images, and Encounters

Forebear to judge, for we are sinners all.

Close his eyes and draw the curtain close;

And let us all to meditation.

— SHAKESPEARE, *King Henry VI*

Nature inspires us, and surely can be an important teacher, but equally important are the words and images we have available to us from great literature both sacred and secular. Having engaged the sense world deeply, we can turn to words, images, and encounters as worthy subjects for meditation. These too can evoke ideas and feelings in us that are well suited to contemplative engagement. Many of the features of sense-based meditation can beneficially be carried over to contemplative work with words, images, and human encounters.

Once when I was sixteen I entered my English class and saw written on the blackboard, "All violence is not power but the absence of power." At the time I did not have a clue what the passage meant, and the teacher wisely refused to enlighten us. For years this aphorism would periodically pop into my mind, contracted into the phrase, "Violence is the absence of power." I would turn it round and round in my mind to see if I could make sense of it. At some point dawn broke, and I began to see clearly the truth that, until then, I had only dimly sensed. To this day this simple sentence has stuck with me. Only recently did I discover that it originates with Ralph Waldo Emerson, but by then I had come to recognize the deep wisdom its words contain. Violence is borne of fear and reveals the absence of true power, for genuine power never requires violence but is always gentle, healing, and loving. Not understanding is essential to discovery. Words have mystery in them; they can enchant us for years even if we do not know what they mean. Think of your favorite poem—do you really understand it?

Meditation on Words

Meditation on a short sentence is perhaps the easiest place to begin word-based contemplative practice. Sentences suitable for meditation should be formed in a way that leads us beyond the prosaic considerations of conventional life. The words, often drawn from sacred texts or poetry, lift us from the usual rounds of thought and speech to deeper reflections. As an example, we can work with the sentence, "There is no fear in love."[92] In meditating on the words of this sentence we are called to contemplate the relationship between these two deep-seated features of the human psyche. More than any outer force, these real but intangible components of our world have determined the actions of peoples through all time.

"There is no fear in love." Meditation on these words can begin by simply sounding the sentence whole, without analysis or a search for meaning. We need not know who wrote the line or under what conditions, because we are not performing a literary deconstruction. On the contrary, we will use these few words purely for the cultivation of soul. While understanding is valuable, it only serves another purpose—transformation. For this reason, it is far more important to *feel* fear and love than to understand them. The words are to work on the imagination and not on the intellect; they are to involve the whole human being, heart and mind. Study is an essential preliminary to meditation, but scholarship, even on esoteric matters, is no replacement for earnest exercise. Sound the sentence again: "There is no fear in love." With each repetition hear it fresh, as if listening for the first time to its parts and its puzzles. Allow it to mystify you for a while before digging deeper.

---

92. 1 John 4:18.

In the next phase of the meditation one can focus on individual words: fear and love, for example. What does fear evoke? Can you find fear in yourself? If not at first, then think of a fearful situation. At this point and throughout the meditation, mental pictures can be a helpful addition to the words. Maybe you felt fear when standing before another person, or when lost in a forest. Do not only think the situation, but feel it as well. Allow the fear to resurface so you know it from the inside. Do not allow yourself to be distracted by irrelevant aspects of the situation. Exactly why were you fearful? Can you trace events backwards to the concern that caused the fear? When lost, was it the prospect of hunger, cold, and possibly even death that caused fear? When standing in front of another person, were you afraid of being ridiculed or humiliated? The prospect of physical or psychological harm can produce fear. Within the fear, we feel that toward which it points. We directly perceive the fear in us, but through it we discover its source beyond us.

In meditation two parts of us are active. What we can call the mind or soul experiences the emotion; in this example, fear. But another part of us, a "meta-consciousness" or higher self, can observe the entire process, at least if we are not overwhelmed or paralyzed by the emotions we feel. Scholars have suggested that the ancient Greeks experienced this higher self outwardly, as the manifestation of a god. In the *Iliad*, for example, when Achilles and Agamemnon were arguing over a slave girl, the goddess Athena appeared and stilled the hand of Achilles as he reached for his sword. In Homer's words,

> Now as he [Achilles] weighed in mind and spirit these two courses
> and was drawing from its scabbard the great sword, Athena descended
> from the sky...
> The goddess standing behind Peleus' son caught him by the fair hair,
> appearing to him only, for no man of the others saw her.[93]

Achilles had paused to weigh in his mind and spirit the action he was about to commit. His premeditation was a call to the gods for guidance.

---

93. Homer, *The Iliad*, trans. Richard Lattimore (Chicago: University of Chicago Press, 1967), Book I, lines 194ff.

With Achilles' hair in her hand, Pallas Athena appeared to him alone and stopped him from killing his noble kinsman.

Today a higher self can become active privately in us and calm our emotional reactions to insult or injury. No longer experienced as a vision of a goddess, this higher self is active in our reflections and meditative work. Our work with this higher nature connects us with realms that reach far beyond the immediate circumstances within which we live. While feeling fear and sensing its immediate root cause, observe also that you can remain at some remove from the inner turmoil and act in the light of a greater wisdom. If the preparatory exercises on control of emotion have been done, then this experience should be readily accessible.

We repeat the words again: "There is no fear in love." From fear we turn to love. This small word with multiple meanings evokes a quite different feeling in us than fear. As before, call to mind the experience of love in your life as a valuable starting point. Love may be given or received. It may involve a parent, grandmother, child, or spouse, or we can selflessly love a favorite place, poem, or piece of music. Each instance of love offers us a means to cultivate one aspect of the experience of love. Allow the experience to well up within you, giving it the time it needs to be truly felt. Ask yourself, "What is the place of fear in love?" Have you ever loved another person who frightens you? It happens. Have you ever loved a place in nature whose immensity provoked fear? Sure. Recognizing these emotions in us suggests the further question, "Can I go deeper in my experience of love to a place where fear loses its force?"

Two images come to mind in which I see no fear in love. The first is the archetypal image of mother and child, appearing in countless depictions of Isis and Horus, as well as of the Madonna and child so familiar in Christian iconography. The child is tenderly held on the lap of the loving mother. The child's future trials and death are held at bay for a time by the all-encompassing love of the mother. No fear can penetrate her protective embrace. No physical or psychic trauma can enter this sphere. The child is the innocent beneficiary of pure love. Like the child, we can all be the unconscious recipient of love and unknowingly enjoy its warm, protective embrace. Living with the image of a child in the arms of his or her loving mother can help us to experience the feeling of "no fear in love." We can be the beloved child.

The infant can be blissfully ignorant of all harmful agencies while in a mother's arms: not so with us. We know the dangers all around us, and imagine others. Like the blacksmith, we learn to respect the heat of fire. We do not turn a blind eye to danger. Therefore a second image is needed, one that represents to us the love we can feel even when confronted with unavoidable threats. I am referring to an image such as that of Mahatma Gandhi's assassination. It was the sixth attempt on his life by Hindu extremists. The assassin, Nathuram Godse, was known to Gandhi from previous attempts. Gandhi had even invited Godse to spend eight days with him so he might better understand Godse's fundamentalist views. The invitation was rebuffed. Although the threat was clear to him, Gandhi refused additional security protection. On that final evening in January 1948, he walked to prayers with the aid of his two helpers, Abha and Manu. One week before he had told Manu, "if someone shot at me and I received his bullet in my bare chest without a sigh and with Rama's [God's] name on my lips, only then should you say that I was a true Mahatma."[94] As Nathuram Godse approached him Gandhi bowed with his hands together in the traditional Hindu greeting, and Godse shot him three times in the chest. As the blood stained his white woolen shawl Gandhi spoke the blessed name of his god, "Hey Ram, Hey Ram," blessing his assassin as he fell to the floor. Only forgiveness was in Gandhi's heart as an answer to the zealous hatred within Godse's. Neither violence nor death caused Gandhi to fear. He was a Mahatma indeed, and knew firsthand that there is no fear in love. Gandhi exemplified the fearless lover who practices forgiveness. The protection granted to the child is put aside; danger is recognized; but the mother's love is internalized, and in this way we change from the beloved to the lover. As lover we carry with us the blue mantle of peace and the red stole of compassion, and we learn from love how to live without fear even in the face of suffering and death.

When meditating a sentence I find that its meaning and power are enhanced by joining images to the words. For example, in the picture of the innocent child on his or her mother's lap I see before me "no fear." In its whole being the child shows no fear, radiating instead a sense of joy and

---

94. Vinay Lal, "'Hey Ram': The Politics of Gandhi's Last Words," *Humanscape*, vol. 8, no. 1 (January 2001), pp. 34–38.

security. "Loving" is depicted for me by the mother herself. She expresses love through the tender way she looks at and holds the infant on her lap. Speaking the words "no fear" while holding the image of the child in mind intensifies the practice. Likewise, combining the word "loving" with the image of the mother helps to strengthen the practice. That not all mothers are loving, and that children can be fearful, is of no consequence. We simply seek a momentary image in which the archetype of "no fear in love" becomes perceptible. In that momentary insight the idea and the image energetically reinforce each other. In an analogous way, the image of Gandhi's assassination presents us with the archetype of the individual who has internalized love, who dwells in love and thereby can meet all adversities without fear. That Gandhi had human failings is of no consequence, because we seek a moment through which a pure manifestation of love without fear can show itself. At the heart of nonviolence lies the infinite power of love that Gandhi practiced. Emerson was right; violence is the absence of power. The converse is also true; the true spiritual power of love reveals itself in the absence of violence and in acts of forgiveness.

Having meditatively lived in the words and images, I inwardly speak the words once again. I hear them echoed back to me from the wide expanses of space: "There is no fear in love." Then I shift the direction of my will, soften it, and open the gate leading to deep silence. Stepping into peace, I allow emptiness to make its reply. Not seeking, not hoping, I wait in a manner that can welcome all things.

Above, I used as my example a line from the Epistles of John, but secular poetry or prose can offer us rich material for meditation as well. When the German poet Novalis writes "Light is the genius of the fire process. Light makes fire," is he not inviting us to meditate? How is it that light makes fire? In what way is light the higher inspiring genius of the fire process? Can I see and feel the candle flame as the consequence of light and not the agent of its production? Words held in contemplative awareness offer us a horizon toward which we can expand. If we give them the time they require to unfold their inherent magic, we grow by reaching out to their larger meanings.

We may also take up a longer verse for meditation. At first, such verses can seem overwhelming. They appear to be too long to take into our meditative life in any reasonable way. We can begin by simply reading a long verse slowly and reflectively. Contemplative reading is highly satisfying. Soon, however, we will want to go deeper. I proceed by selecting a single line from the verse as my beginning. One can meditate it as I have described above, word by word, phrase by phrase. That one line becomes a microcosm of the whole. Over time other lines can be added so that gradually we create a relationship with the entire verse. Each line can then resound with a depth that a simple reading cannot offer. After such work line by line, reading the whole verse slowly and reflectively, pausing at the end of every phrase and line, can draw us deeply into the full power of the verse in its entirety.

The Word in Christian Meditation

The mystery and power of words has been acknowledged by all contemplative traditions. While we may associate mantric meditation with Asian traditions, the Christian West has long had a custom of meditative reading, reflection, and prayer whose stages are much like those I have described. In recent years "centering prayer" has become a simple but powerful means of using a single word as a means of orienting toward the sacred. The method is very similar to some of the practices we have undertaken. Its roots extend back to the Desert Fathers and Mothers of the first centuries of Christianity, and to the classic contemplative text *The Cloud of Unknowing*. Centering prayer consists of four steps that in total take twenty minutes or so.[95] As explained by cofounder Rev. Thomas Keating,

1. We choose a sacred word that symbolizes our intention to invite God's presence into ourselves. The word might be Abba, Mother, Peace, Shalom, or Love, for example.
2. Sitting silently with eyes closed, we allow the mind to settle and then introduce the sacred word into the center of our attention.
3. If we become aware of distracting thoughts or feelings, we pause and gently return to the word.
4. At the close of the prayer we remain silent for two or three minutes.

---

95. See www.centeringprayer.com for background and detailed instruction.

In centering prayer we endow a single word with the potential to awaken us to spiritual presence. While the choice of word is significant, of far greater significance is the quality of attention we bring to it. Notice that centering prayer also makes use of focused attention and silent, open awareness. It calls these two stages of practice by their Latin names: *meditatio* and *contemplatio*.

The Benedictine order has practiced *lectio divina* for centuries.[96] In the twelfth century William of St. Thierry likened the difference between *lectio divina* and casual reading to that between a true friendship and the acquaintance we have with a passing guest.[97] In *lectio divina* we befriend the text before us, deepening our relationship to it in stages. The first of the four stages is *lectio*, which means both reading and listening. In this stage a selection from scripture is read slowly as we "listen with the ear of the heart," to use St. Benedict's words. Intellectual understanding alone is insufficient. The heart welcomes the emotional content of the passage; it is the organ of empathetic knowing. The second stage is *meditatio*, or meditation, in which we take a short selection from the full reading as the subject for deep reflection. In the previous example we took, "There is no fear in love." We ponder words such as these in the heart and connect them to our personal feelings and aspirations. That of which scripture speaks is seen to have direct pertinence to our own lives. Scripture is viewed as the archetype of which our personal struggles are instances.

The third stage of *lectio divina* is called *oratio*, or prayer. In this stage we choose something out of our life, perhaps a difficult experience, and use the words of our meditation to consecrate or heal that experience. If we have felt fear, we can recall that instance and hold it in our awareness, surrounding it with love until the fear is dissolved. Within the Christian meditative tradition, the selected passage is a means by which God is invited into the heart in order to bless and aid the petitioner. The final stage is *contemplatio* or contemplation. Here we cultivate complete

---

96. Fr. Luke Dysinger, "Accepting the Embrace of God: The Ancient Art of *Lectio Divina*," in *The Art and Vocation of Caring for People in Pain*, Karl A. Schultz (Paulist Press, 1993), pp. 98–110; or http://www.valyermo.com/ld-art.html.
97. William of St. Thierry, *The Golden Epistle*, trans. Theodore Berkeley (Spencer, MA: Cisterian Publications, 1971), pp. 51–52 or www.osb.org/lectio/thierry.html.

wordless silence and foster a communion with the presence of God. Thus through the practice of *lectio divina* we take up a sacred text and give a selected passage our full meditative attention. We bring the passage into relationship with the specific realities of our life, seeking assistance and blessing. Finally, we end with silent contemplation, openness to the presence of spirit.

Meditation on Images

Just as the mystery and power of words are universally appreciated, so too is the potency of images recognized by many cultures. Of course, images are not just an aid in our word meditations but have a power all their own. Our culture is suffused with images that are showered on us by every form of media. Within traditional cultures the production of an image was a deed that required skill, special materials, and effort. A Buddhist thangka painting, a Greek sculpture, or the head mask of an African society presents community members with a means to move beyond mundane consciousness. Navajo sand painting is a powerful example of the use of image within traditional societies, and the manner of its production and use can help us to understand the methods of meditating on images today.

Navajo legend relates that sand painting was a gift from their gods, whom the Navajo called "Holy People." While the Holy People were able to draw sacred images in the sky, the Navajo Singers (shamans) were instructed to compose their images using sand, colored stone powder, pollen, and similar natural substances. Unlike framed paintings that hang in today's art museums, Navajo sand paintings were intended to be used, and their primary function was and remains healing.

When a person is suffering illness or distress he or she seeks out the traditional Navajo Singer, who diagnoses the problem and prescribes the proper song, ceremony, and sand painting (of which there are approximately 1000). The ceremony of chanting and ritual can last up to nine days, and includes production of a large sand painting. It is composed of symbolic renderings drawn from Navajo life, including stories of the Holy People, and depicts a Way or story though which the Singer leads his patient. In response to the Singer's call, certain of the Holy People (gods) are invited to enter the painting through the opening on its eastern side. The name in Navajo for the paintings literally means the "place where the gods come and go." At the climax of the ceremony the patient is seated by the Singer in the center of the painting and rubbed with the pigments. In other words he or she enters and inhabits for a time the sacred imaginal world of the painting, becoming fully part of it and the story it tells. The patient who was ill or "out of balance," who had in the Navajo view lost the beauty of well-being or *hózhó*, is restored to beauty. The words chanted by the Singer might include,

> Dark cloud is at the door.
> The trail out of it is dark cloud.
> The zigzag lightning stands high upon it.
> An offering I make.
> Restore my feet for me.
> Restore my legs for me.
> Restore my body for me.
> Restore my mind for me.
> Restore my voice for me.
> This very day take out your spell for me.[98]

Then the sand painting is destroyed, its elements returned to Mother Earth. The painting came into being for a task, and with the completion of that task the painting is dispersed.

The tradition of sand mandalas (from the Sanskrit word meaning circle) is common to Hindu and Buddhist religions, and is similar in many respects to that found in the Navajo tradition. The creation of these complex images is an intentional act that in itself is believed to bring blessing. As with the Navajo, once the use of the sand mandala has been fulfilled it is destroyed, thereby showing the impermanence of all things. Here too, those who work with the mandala understand that it is a depiction of a spiritual reality into which the monk journeys. The two-dimensional mandala image is made into a three-dimensional landscape in the monk's

---

98. Taken from http://www.1stholistic.com/Spl_prayers/prayer_navaho-chant.htm.

imagination. The mandala becomes a Way that leads the meditator through sacred precincts to demons and gods, each of which the monk is to know from the inside by living into their forms, activities, and meanings.

In both of the above traditions, Native American and Asian, we can identify three parts to the work with image. The seeker must construct the image, then work with or live into it deeply, and finally release it. These traditional elements reappear in modern meditation on images. The first part of the meditation entails building up the image in the mind. Once created so that it is vividly before one, the image is engaged actively in some way. At the conclusion one closes the meditation with gratitude, releasing the image while holding one's attention open for a time afterward.

Selecting an image suited for meditation is quite personal. What is right for one person can sometimes offend another. Sacred images are rooted deeply in the traditions from which they come. If you are a practicing Christian then the images from Native American cultures or the Jewish Tree of Life, which is central to the Kabala, may be inaccessible or inappropriate. Each spiritual lineage has developed its own specialized iconographic language with explicit and implicit reference to the lineage's stories, sages, and deities. The Orthodox Church makes intensive use of icons depicting the Christian saints and martyrs, while Tibetan *tanka* paintings present the Buddha and the bodhisattvas in a remarkable formal system of symbolic representations. To a Buddhist practitioner an icon of St. Joseph amid his carpenter's tools is meaningless, and to an Orthodox meditant a depiction of Avalokiteshvara with eleven faces and eight hands is likewise without significance. We should also be mindful of those traditions that shun images as idols that too easily usurp the unimaginable nature of the divine. Yet each of us can find images that speak our language of soul and are well suited to our spiritual striving. Finding such images may take some searching, but that is part of the practice as well.

Secular Images

For instructional purposes, I introduce an image meditation based on one given by Rudolf Steiner to curative educators, one that uses only a simple geometrical figure. Such a diagram, with few or no religious associations, can yet be highly effective.[99] To begin, we create in our minds a circle, imagining it as vividly as possible. We then imagine the circle slowly shrinking, becoming smaller and smaller until it becomes a single point. Then make the point expand again into a circle that grows to the size of the one we first drew. The transformation can be repeated several times so that we can feel the process of contraction and expansion as we change the circle into a point and the point back into a circle. Sense the difference between point and periphery.

The exercise can be taken further by modifying the diagram so that a single point is at the center of the circle from the outset. From here we will try to imagine both movements taking place simultaneously: the circle contracts as the point expands. This is difficult because it requires us to think two opposite thoughts at the same time. Once again we recall Nicolas of Cusa's coincidence of opposites. To keep the movements distinct, we can color the outer circle blue and the center point yellow. At the same time as the blue circle contracts, we allow the central yellow point to expand until the two change places. We now have a yellow circle surrounding a blue point. What was outer becomes inner, and what was inner becomes outer. We should slowly repeat the movements of simultaneous expansion and contraction until the rhythmic exchange of exterior for interior is felt inwardly. We may note with special appreciation the unique moment when the two circles pass through one another. In that instant there is no difference between them, and in the next moment they exchange roles. Feel the distinct characters of the exterior circle and the central point. If you are having difficulty, imagine you are watching a group of dancers from a high balcony. Half of the dancers (dressed in blue) are in the outer circle while the other half (dressed in yellow) are grouped tightly together at the center. As the blue group moves in, the yellow group moves out. You are able to see both happening at the same time. Then the blue group moves out, and the yellow moves back in. Having mastered the dancers, return to the circles and try again.

The experience of point and periphery, which this simple exercise stimulates, is quite far-reaching. This polarity can be found everywhere

---

99. Rudolf Steiner, *Curative Education*, trans. Mary Adams (London: Rudolf Steiner Press, 1972), pp. 178-179, 201–202.

that expansion and contraction appear; for example, in the two phases of breathing, or in the growth of the plant expanding from the seed into leaves and then contracting back to the flower bud. In the exercise we can also feel the relationship between center and periphery that echoes throughout history as the relationship between the macrocosm and the microcosm. The two paths of self development reflect these polar processes. One path takes the seeker out into the wide expanses of the world while the other leads her deep into the self. The exercise mirrors our movement between two poles: to the divine in the cosmos and to the divine within. In Rudolf Steiner's description of this practice he connects two short phrases with the two figures. When the blue circle surrounds the yellow point he suggests the words, "God is in me." When the yellow point has expanded to become the outer circle and the blue becomes a point, then he suggests the words, "I am in God."

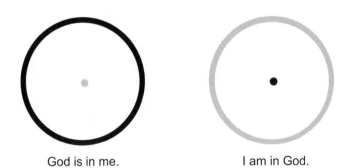

God is in me.   I am in God.

Practicing the metamorphosis of point into periphery and back again can change the way we think. One example is the difference between what I term "peripheral planning" and "central planning." In all aspects of life, we are accustomed to plan ahead, to work toward objectives. We generally work from our center out. We are central planners. The stream of thought and action starts with me, and I shape the world according to my will and ideas. Think of formal French gardens or a quarterback yelling to his team. Both are willful impositions of ideas, on nature in one case and on players in the other. But English gardeners have a different ethic, and so do jazz musicians. Sometimes far more interesting and intelligent things happen if we drop the attempt to plan everything centrally and become attentive instead to the periphery. Other people may have something to offer me; they also have ideas and intentions, after all. Maybe we should learn to improvise more and plan less. The next time you step into a meeting, turn to others; attend to them first, asking what the world has in store for you. The teachings of Socrates and Jesus seem almost exclusively to occur in response to sudden chance meetings or events. Contrast their spontaneity with the staging of a political campaign with its strategic plans and implementation efforts, or the roll-out of a new commercial product. All the great sages seem to have been peripheral planners, not central planners. Judging by the endurance of their ideas and impulses, peripheral planning seems to have much to recommend it. Valuing the periphery becomes especially significant if, as many spiritual traditions maintain, the universe itself is a place of agency, wisdom, and even moral guidance. If we are awake to the wide circle of reality around us, then its intelligence can join to ours in ways that reach far beyond what we can imagine from our point-wise awareness.

Meditating the continuous exchange of point and periphery is a purely secular exercise. Image exercises of a more explicitly spiritual character often trigger justified antipathies because of association with heinous groups that have captured them. The ancient Chinese "wan," for example, can no longer be used since the design was taken and perverted by the Nazis into the symbol we know as the swastika. For many, the atrocities perpetrated by the Spanish Inquisition and the Ku Klux Klan have turned the Christian cross from a symbol of sacrifice and rebirth into one of oppression. This being said, it is nevertheless true that the meditation on point and circle can be considerably enhanced by adding to it symbolic elements drawn from nature. What follows is one variant of Rudolf Steiner's rose-cross meditation.[100]

At the center of the image, for example, one can place a fire, complete with glowing wooden embers, ash, and smoke as well as light and heat. It can be for us the fire of transformation and purification to which we give ourselves in meditation. The circle can become a braided circle of

---

100. Rudolf Steiner, *The Secret Stream*, ed. Christopher Bamford (Great Barrington, MA: Anthroposophic Press, 2000), p. 244.

seven red roses. Let us imagine roses approaching the center from the distant reaches of space, each bringing with it a particular gift or virtue. The fire burns away the impure in us and opens us outward, making us ready to receive inspiration. We can begin by viewing the image of roses as if in front of us, but soon it becomes evident that we should enter the image. Like the Navajo, we should move inside the painting. We take our place at the center, standing upright with our arms (mentally) outstretched, forming a cross. The fire burns within us at the place of the heart, the crossing point of our uprightness and our outstretched arms, but it also consumes all that should perish to be reborn in us. Arrayed around us are the seven red roses, each of which brings a spiritual gift. We turn first to the rose on the left side of our head; it becomes radiant, and we gratefully receive from it the gift of *warmth*.

Feeling the warmth, we then turn to the right side and gratefully receive from the luminous second rose the gift of *light*. We linger to receive the second gift rightly. By our left hand the third rose brightens and brings *wakefulness*, and on the right side the fourth brings *peace*. Below on the left hovers a rose bringing *strength* in life, and by the right foot is a rose that brings us the forces of new life or *renewal*. We gratefully accept these gifts also. Six radiant roses surround us: three illuminating the left, and three illuminating the right. Two hover beside the head, two beside the heart, two beside our feet. The radiant presence of each rose is felt, and each gift is affirmed and accepted: warmth, light, wakefulness, peace, strength, and renewal. Finally, a rose descends directly above us, coming to rest over our head. Sensing the light of the final rose completing the circle, we say, "I am in your domain." We sustain the moment, living for a time within the sphere of the seven luminous rose presences, and then, with gratitude in our heart, we release them. We extinguish the fire, so that at the end we are inwardly quiet and at peace, open to all things.

In this meditation, we combine the openness represented by the inner fire, whose light and warmth radiate outward, with the in-streaming gifts of the spirit carried to us by the roses. We internalize the gifts around us, and carry out into the periphery what is noble in us. We can live for some minutes in the presence and power of these images, allowing them to work on us. The closing is familiar to us by now, and so we find our way to open awareness and deep inner peace. With gratitude, we turn back to life.

Situation Meditation

A natural extension of word and image meditation is what I term "situation meditation." In this type of meditation one inwardly enters imaginatively into a dramatic situation that is intended to provide a spiritual teaching or to rehearse a particular spiritual situation. Many traditional teaching tales can be appreciated on the level of a simple story, but they may also depict important stages of one's contemplative journey worthy of deeper attention. For example, the *Norwegian Dream Song of Olaf Åsteson* recounts the long dream that Olaf Åsteson had during the twelve Holy Nights between Christmas and Epiphany. The stages of the dream song are also the stages through which the individual passes via meditative self-development. For instance, when on the fourth day of his dream Olaf reaches the Gjaller Bridge, he is confronted by three beasts: the serpent, the hound, and the bull.

> The serpent strikes and the fierce hound bites,
> The bull stands ready to ram me—
> None will pass over the Gjaller heights
> Who with judgment false have damned.
> The moon shines bright
> And the paths were far to follow.[101]

We meet here a rendering of an archetypal threshold situation. The bridge across the abyss marks a fundamental shift in consciousness and is associated with a confrontation of the self in its different aspects. While the imagery depicts them attacking from the outside, the three beasts are within us. In order to cross the Gjaller bridge, that which was buried in our subconscious mind must be raised to full wakeful awareness. The beasts are the untransformed faculties of thinking, feeling, and willing in us. We must be fully master of ourselves before crossing the Gjaller Bridge connecting two otherwise distinct worlds of awareness.

---

101. *The Dream Song of Olaf Åsteson*, trans. Eleanor C. Merry (East Grinstead, England: New Knowledge Books, 1961), p. 22.

Such stories are far too long to meditate one word or symbol at a time. We can, however, live our way into the drama, into the situation. We become Olaf Åsteson and live through his actions and experiences in our imagination. We join him on the first day as he "wandered above the cloudy height / and plunged in bottomless waters" or later as he struggles through the thicket of thorns to the abyss over which the Gjaller Bridge arches. Each stage of the journey is lived imaginatively. In each of the previous exercises, we practiced participation; here we do the same but on a larger and richer scale.

The classic texts on which this form of imaginative meditation can be practiced are innumerable. Thomas à Kempis and countless Christian monks practiced participatory meditation in the life, passion, and death of Christ as the model which they meditated. The Stations of the Cross are a ritualized form in which the Catholic faithful practice situation meditation. In Hinduism the conversation between Arjuna and his charioteer, Krishna, recorded in the *Bhagavad-Gita* has been the object not only of study and reflection but of meditation as well. One can, with great profit, take the stages of Odysseus's journey home as the content of situation meditations. In ancient Egyptian myth, the goddess Isis, having lost her husband Osiris to the demon Set (Gk. Typhon), brings him back to life by finding the parts of his dismembered body. Her fidelity rejuvenates the dead. In each case, we should enter into the situation of the various characters, becoming for a time the wise charioteer, the beleaguered warrior, the loving spouse; meeting the tests of the spiritual journey in each case.

In addition to working with stories in this way, longer poems and meditative verses are very often best treated as situation meditations. This may require some imagination because there may be no human character in the verse with whom we can identify. The guiding principle remains: participation in the drama with our thoughts, feelings, and imagination. As before, one should be careful to remain centered, awake, and aware throughout. Our goal is not a lapse into romantic reverie, an emotional "high," or the sensation of blissful union. This meditation is a schooling of the inner life that enhances our sensitivities and nuances our sensibilities through fuller participation in the sense world—the world of image and word—but should never lead to dreamy detachment or emotional indulgence. Eventually this practice leads us to a way of knowing that yields insights as valuable as any of those given us by science.

As an example of a verse that can be taken up in this way, consider the "Peace Dance," a verse given by Rudolf Steiner to a group of eurythmists in 1924.

> The wishes of the soul are quickened,
> The deeds of the will wax and grow,
> The fruits of life are ripening.
>
> I feel my fate,
> My fate finds me.
> I feel my star,
> My star finds me.
> I feel my aims,
> My aims find me.
> My soul and the world are one.
>
> Life will be clearer around me,
> Life will be more burdensome for me,
> Life will be richer for me.
>
> Strive for Peace,
> Live in Peace,
> Love Peace.[102]

The verse is too long to hold within us at once in its entirety. We can, however, move through it, building up for ourselves each line and section. We can feel the soul striving to become enlivened. Our actions should grow stronger, and our lives should ripen. The second stanza brings us into the stream of destiny, and we affirm the feelings of guidance that can fill us in meditation. In this way we live, line by line, into the world of the verse. It is like an elaborate sand painting with many colors, forms, and symbols.

---

102. Rudolf Steiner, *Eurythmy as Visible Speech*, (London: Rudolf Steiner Press, 1984) July 10, 1924.

Their significance may not be immediately available to us, but through contemplative engagement we are nurtured by them, grow together with them, and come to an ever fuller insight into their meanings.

Contemplative Encounters

> *We'll not reach the goal one*
>
> *by one but in pairs.*
>
> — PAUL ELUARD, "OUR LIFE"[103]

Once, when I was talking about healing and teaching with the physician, educator, and author Rachel Naomi Remen, our conversation turned to meditation. She said that her practice did not take place on a cushion or with her eyes closed; rather, it took place looking into the eyes of her patients and into the fears of those who face death. Each meeting, each conversation, each illness is an occasion for deep stillness, empathetic listening, and compassionate healing. She brings contemplative awareness to her encounters, and they become transformative both for her and those she cares for.

I am not suggesting that we should walk through life meditating. In fact I believe that the time we take for practice should be segregated from the bustle of normal life. We set aside time to practice a musical instrument or athletic skill. The cultivation of a wider and more insightful form of consciousness must, likewise, be given its own time and space. That said, life presents us with many opportunities to bring the special capacities we have cultivated into service. The stillness and open awareness we have become so familiar with in meditation can be brought with benefit to conversations with partners, students, patients, business associates, and clients. The quality of attention we bring can directly influence the level and tone of the meeting. It can profoundly change the doctor-patient relationship, even the relation between lawyer and client. Law

---

103. Translation copyright A.S. Kline, 2001.

professor Leonard Riskin has thoroughly documented the significant role that meditation can play in legal negotiations, and his work has been the centerpiece of a Harvard symposium on dispute resolution.[104]

Our meetings with others can be a repeated occasion for the cultivation of meditative attention. If we are sufficiently practiced in cultivating the meditative state of mind, then taking a few breaths, settling into ourselves and attending gently, openly, and completely to the other is usually sufficient for a recognizable inner shift to take place. We drop the combative stance, we live into the thoughts of the other, and so are practicing a form of selfless attention. We need not correct what may be mistakes of fact or differences of opinion. In this moment we are positive and open to the other. What we achieved in our preliminary solitary exercises becomes of practical use in relationships. In my experience, the visual background surrounding my conversation partner fades, and the face and voice of the partner are all that remains. Everything extraneous seems to fall away. The exchange can even take on a joyful, sacramental character as a mutual recognition of the divine within each other silently arises.

Martin Buber has written of the profound change in relationship that is possible when we move from I-It to I-Thou.[105] In that moment, what had been an object or "It" becomes a subject or "Thou." In our previous meditations on nature, the effort was made to convert nature's objects into subjects. In the language of naturalist-philosopher David Abram, we discover that the world of critters is looking back, indeed everything is looking back at us.[106] This was exactly how the Nobel biologist Barbara McClintock spoke about her maize plants.[107] Her biographer Evelyn Fox Keller observed how McClintock's relationship to corn had become

---

104. Leonard Riskin, "The Contemplative Lawyer: On the Potential Relevance of Mindfulness Meditation to Law Students, Lawyers, and their Clients," *Harvard Negotiation Law Review* (May 2002), the centerpiece of a Harvard University symposium entitled *Mindfulness in Law and Dispute Resolution*, http://www.pon.harvard.edu/news/2002/riskin_mindfulness.php3.

105. Martin Buber, *I and Thou*, trans. Walter Kaufmann (New York: Charles Scribner's, 1970).

106. David Abram, *The Spell of the Sensuous* (New York: Vintage Books, 1997).

107. Evelyn Fox Keller, *A Feeling for the Organism: The Life and Work of Barbara McClintock*, (New York: W. H. Freeman, 1984).

that of one subject (herself) empathetically knowing another subject (the corn). The corn plants seemed to speak back to her.

The primatologist Jane Goodall had to wait patiently for six months before the chimpanzees she sought to study became accustomed to her presence. As she waited, she recalled the advice of her mentor, Louis Leakey; if she was calm and meant no harm to the animals they would sense it and would not harm her. In her book *Resaon for Hope*, Goodall recounts how she found a profound peace in the jungle. Her long sessions, waiting and observing in every kind of weather, became a form of meditation. She sensed a great power in the bush, far more easily than she had in London. In her book, Goodall reported: "I and the chimpanzees, the earth and trees and air, seemed to merge, to become one with the spirit power of life itself." Gradually the chimpanzees allowed her to come closer. Her intimacy with them, born of gentleness and patience, permitted her to make observations that soon revolutionized the field of primatology. Martin Buber characterized such relationships in these words: "I-Thou is a relationship of openness, directness, mutuality, and presence. It may be between man and man, but may also take place with a tree, a cat, a piece of mica, a work of art—and through all of these with God, the 'eternal Thou' in whom the parallel lines of relations meet."

In such moments of true I-Thou encounter, especially those that arise through our meetings with other persons, we meet the sacred. In light of McClintock, Goodall, and Buber, we can understand Steiner's words when he speaks about the future, saying,[108]

> In the future every human being shall see a hidden divinity in each and every fellow human being. Then there will be no need for religious coercion, for every meeting between one person and another will be of itself in the nature of a religious rite, a sacrament.

True meetings have a sacramental character. Contemplative practice and its accompanying moral development can move us toward the

---

108. Rudolf Steiner, October 9, 1918. "The Working of the Angel in Man's Astral Body." See also Athys Floride, *The Human Encounter* and Rudolf Steiner, *Interesse für den Anderen Menschen* (Stuttgart: Verlag Freies Geistesleben, 1999).

possibility of true human encounters, to meetings where the core reality of the person across from us is more fully present before and within us. When this occurs, something intangible is sensed and exchanged. We live for a moment together in the world formed by our mutual attending.

CHAPTER SIX

Contemplative Cognition

All absolute perception is religious.

— NOVALIS

At a scientific conference on consciousness, the psychologist Charles Tart performed an informal survey of those present. He first described an archetypal transcendent experience, based on accounts given to him while doing research at UC Davis. His description sounded not unlike Emerson's experience of becoming a "transparent eyeball" through which the currents of the world passed. He spoke of feeling enveloped by light; selfless, radically interconnected, and open to the new experience in which self and world are one. Then he asked how many had had an experience of this kind during their lifetime. Perhaps forty percent of those present raised their hands.

After giving a talk at Brown University on the place of contemplative practice in higher education, I had a private conversation with a physicist there who was also a Zen practitioner. We certainly had a common starting point in physics, but as we continued to talk about meditation something important became evident. As with so many others, for him meditation was not a spiritual practice. Rather, it offered clear psychological benefits, and that was sufficient. He had specifically sought out a form of practice that largely avoided metaphysical or religious trappings. His daily practice alone was the important factor. There is something attractive about this attitude. The history of the West as well as the East is littered with squabbles and wars fought over doctrinal differences concerning the "true nature of the divine." We have learned that those disputes were mostly due to the diverse cultural and social contexts in which the different religious traditions developed. The disputes, in other words, had little or nothing to do with God, and had everything to do with the idiosyncrasies of our own ways of representing experience or interpreting scripture.

I respect the position taken by my Brown colleague, and his principled stance is one common to many thoughtful practitioners. Mindfulness practices, such as attending to the breath, learning to be present in the moment, and cultivating loving-kindness, bring genuine benefit to the practitioner. Why ask for more? The problem is that even if one doesn't ask for more, more often shows up. Subtle, and sometime not-so-subtle, experiences arise during meditation. What do we make of them? How do we handle them? In Tart's informal survey, most of the experiences reported were spontaneous, that is, they arose without people trying to induce an altered state of awareness. Through meditation the practitioner cultivates a form of awareness that inclines him or her to transcendent experiences of one kind or another. Once one takes up meditation, experiences arise.

In light of such considerations, and because of my many conversations with practitioners who are skeptical about spirituality, I would like to suggest a way of proceeding that requires no metaphysical commitments. It does, however, permit one to remain open-minded in the long term about the nature of meditative experience and its possible usefulness. This way of proceeding is also valuable for those who meditate with explicitly spiritual aspirations, offering them some protection against the dangers of projection and egotism. Hence we all need to consider the question of meditative experiences more thoroughly than we have so far.

Towards a Phenomenology of Meditative Experience

In chapter one I described the cautious attitudes of St. John of the Cross and of Buddhist practitioners toward such experiences. St. John felt that spiritual visions were not trustworthy guides to God, and that the only proper attitude was to shun them when they arose (which they certainly did in his case), and to rely instead on faith alone. Buddhists recognize the so-called *siddhis* or psychic powers, treating them as inevitable developments that accompany the meditative life. The experiences associated with the activation of the *siddhis* are considered to be mostly a distraction from the goal of enlightenment. The mental phenomena associated with deep meditation are, in this view, another source of attachment to be seen through and set aside.

Adopting a scientific approach to experiences that arise during meditation is also subject to error because science is always in the danger of assuming a metaphysic. In other words, we are forever presupposing that we know more than we do. The most common metaphysical assumption among scientists today is materialism; others may assert with confidence that everything is mind.[109] We have precious little information that bears directly on the true nature of reality. We possess all kinds of observational and experimental data, and we have theories about the world, but our data and theories are invariably bound to experience. This means that we are never truly free to say what reality is "in itself," but only how it appears to us. At first this seems a great tragedy. The opportunity to solve the mystery of the ultimate nature of things appears to be denied us. We can, however, turn this state of affairs around to our advantage.

The first step is to set aside all metaphysical musing and adopt a positive attitude toward experience. Rather than thinking of our experiences as merely subjective impressions thrown up by the "real world," we set aside all notions of a real world beyond experience and stay with experience itself. At first this may appear to be a view that threatens the very foundations of life. After all, the objects of everyday consciousness are real. But because they too are experienced, they have a safe place in this view. Nothing changes, except our attitude. We cultivate an attitude that values phenomena of all types.

The smell of the red rose, the rustle of a bird in the branches overhead, and all normal sense experiences, of course, remain. But we resist saying to ourselves that these are mere appearances. The iridescent colors on the butterfly's wing are as real as the flower on which it rests. The paramecium

---

109. The Oxford philosopher Michael Lockwood uses this strategy to explain the puzzle of *qualia*, or the fact that things appear to have qualitative properties.

that appears beneath the microbiologist's microscope is real. All phenomena occupy the same space. Not only sense experiences have standing in this view, but feelings, memories, dreams, and all other impressions that rise up in consciousness. In this way, meditative experience can take its place as another legitimate class of conscious impressions. We can become careful observers in the laboratory of our own minds. The phenomena of meditation have exactly as much standing as the phenomena of the physical senses.

Of course, sense impressions tell us about a world largely external to us, and they are essential to a functioning life in that world. I am not advocating a solipsism by which we are imprisoned in our own subjectivity. The outer world is robust and demanding; our friends and foes, our loves and losses, are all around us and remain so. However, by staying close to experience, and thus resisting the urge to project a particular metaphysics onto experience, we remain agnostic about what may or may not stand behind experience. I am suggesting that we take a phenomenological approach to all of our experience, including contemplative experience, in the sense that we stay close to lived experience. Here is not the place to elaborate a full coherent philosophy of experience, but if one stays close to experience and remains agnostic concerning the true nature of reality, that is enough.

Nor are the phenomena of life limited to sense impressions. Our thoughts and feelings likewise form an essential part of our phenomenal domain, but with a difference. While we can both see and smell the rose, my thoughts are private. Yet thoughts and feelings can be shared through language, mathematics, and the arts, and should be granted the same robust standing as other phenomena. How real are our thoughts? Consider, for example, the commitment to democracy. The rise of the democratic ideal in ancient Greece was the victory of an idea over tradition. We continue to hold democracy as a high value, one many are willing to die to preserve against tyranny. Even if as idea such as democracy is imperfectly embodied, it is prized more highly than the rose. I would say that the idea of democracy is real. We know it when we see it, and we also know when it is threatened.

Democracy may order a society, but what orders nature? The phenomena of the sense world are not chaotic, random occurrences, but rather display a marvelous array of patterns in space and time. Science has occupied itself with the exploration and determination of these in enormous detail. I would grant our experience of the lawfulness of nature equal standing, equal reality, with our experience of the sense world. What counts as real in a phenomenological approach of the type I am advocating is not restricted to sense experience but includes mental phenomena as well. In fact, even the rose is, in part, a mental phenomenon, or I would not know it to be a rose. Knowledge is constituted from two sides: in the act of cognition, each percept from the sense world is united to a concept in our minds.[110] In Buddhism, one speaks of cognition as a "co-dependent arising." All physical and mental phenomena are acknowledged to depend on other physical and mental phenomena for their very existence—and hence are considered to have no independent identity at all.

Meditation is another domain of experience. For instance, the luminous calm that meditation can sometimes produce is one of the experiences valued by practitioners. Neuroscientists can monitor the blood flow and neural activity of the brain and tell us the specific neural correlates in the prefrontal cortex that are associated with such positive affective states. While certainly interesting, this does not impact in the slightest on our concerns. We are unconcerned with facts about the brain. Instead we steadily attend to our first-person, lived experiences. As we take up specific contemplative exercises, certain experiences begin to appear. Staying close to the phenomena, we allow them to unfold. We resist the tendency to explain them away as merely brain oscillations, or to imagine them as the visitation of angelic presences. Neither view is admitted. Instead we remain close to the phenomena of meditative life, allowing them their own time and place in our field of attention. For those who know Goethe's approach to the sciences, we are practicing his method of "delicate empiricism," but now on meditative experience in place of plants or colors.[111]

---

110. Rudolf Steiner, *Truth and Knowledge*, trans. Rita Stebbing (Blauvelt, NY: Steiner Books, 1981); *Goethe's Theory of Knowledge: An Outline of the Epistemology of His Worldview,* trans. Peter Clemm (Great Barrington, MA: SteinerBooks, 2008); *Philosophy of Freedom,* trans. Michael Wilson (London: Rudolf Steiner Press, 1964).
111. David Seamon and Arthur Zajonc, *Goethe's Way of Science* (Albany, NY: SUNY Press, 1998).

What is theory's place in all of this? In Goethe's famous words, "The facts themselves are the theory." If we hold to the phenomena, they can gradually become intelligible. We begin to see the relationships and patterns of appearance, and in this way work ourselves up to a high level of perceptive judgment that sees the coherence or meaning in what initially was indecipherable. Remember that the Greek root of the word "theory" means "to behold." This is not to discount the value of study. Others have gone before us on the path of meditation, and their seasoned experience and hard-won insights can be enormously valuable. As long as we never lose our independence, the study of the spiritual traditions of the past, and conversation with those more experienced than we, should be an important part of our practice.

The empirical stance I am advocating was recommended by one of America's greatest philosophers, William James, both in general and specifically with respect to religious experience. For too long, religion had been separated from experience. The contemplative streams of the Western denominations have long been seen as secondary to dogmatic theology as elaborated by means of dialectics. Empiricism has, until now, only been associated with science, which James called irreligious. In place of the dialectical analysis of church doctrines, James saw great promise for religion if it could be associated with empiricism, that is, with meditative experience.[112]

> Let empiricism once become associated with religion, as hitherto, through some strange misunderstanding, it has been associated with irreligion, and I believe that a new era of religion as well as philosophy will be ready to begin.... I fully believe that such an empiricism is a more natural ally than dialectics ever were, or can be, of the religious life.

In what follows, when I present exercises and describe the experiences that sometimes accompany them, I will generally treat the experiences phenomenologically, as described above. However, since I consider phenomena encountered in meditation to be part of a path that can ultimately lead to spiritual insights, I will therefore also occasionally frame

---

112. William James, *A Pluralistic Universe* (Cambridge: Harvard University Press, 1909/ 1979), p. 142.

meditative experience within the language of the spiritual traditions. If the reader is skeptical, he or she can proceed in a completely empirical manner. I am confident that the path we walk in meditation can, over time, offer its own evidence and assurances, as long as we remain truly open-minded. In the end, we will solve the mystery of the ultimate nature of reality not by inference, but through experience.

Cultivating Discernment

When you are arranging flowers in a vase and step back to consider the effect, what are you looking at? When struggling to align the optical elements of a laser system, what am I seeing that guides my fingers until the apparatus is perfectly adjusted? How do you and I know when everything is exactly right? To what are we comparing what we see? We appear to have an ideal in mind, something that can never exist physically but is the standard against which we judge everything. What is the nature of that ideal? Is it real or merely an extrapolation of the mind?

Looking again at the light and colors emitted from the laser, I "see" them as a meaningful whole, as amplified spontaneous emission. From my understanding of the optics of mirrors and a gain medium, I can judge the degree and direction of misalignment, and correct it. My looking is more than mere observing; it is intelligent. My observations and actions are already full of ideas, or "theory-laden," as philosopher N. R. Hanson termed it.[113] The same holds true for any skilled craftsman. Even if they lack the formal theoretical understanding of the physicist, their looking is full of intelligence born of long experience, mistakes, and triumphs. When that intelligence flows unimpeded into their hands, beautiful work appears like ripe fruit on the limb of a pear tree. If that intelligence is lacking, then the phenomena of consciousness convey no meaning at all. The coherence of colors, forms, and sounds vanishes into an inchoate kaleidoscope of impressions.

In *Catching the Light*, I tell the true story of a French child born blind. In 1910, at eight years of age, he was operated on by two doctors, Moreau

---

113. N. R. Hanson, *Patterns of Discovery* (Cambridge: Cambridge University Press, 1965).

and LePrince, and the congenital condition that caused his blindness was removed. Suddenly he was filled with impressions of a world he had known only through his other four senses. What did he see? After removing the bandages from his young patient's eyes, the doctor waved his hand in front of the boy's eyes, but with no noticeable response. The doctor repeated the action several times: nothing. Then suddenly the boy heard the hand's motion as it whished through the air near him, and in a rush saw it as well. Day after day the boy's doctor and nurses worked with him to teach him colors and shapes, helping him with the daunting task of learning to see. Sadly, in the end they failed; the task was simply too difficult. From the study of many such cases, as well as from research on animal vision, we know that learning to see is uniquely possible in the first years of human life. What appears to be natural to the infant is extraordinarily difficult later on. To permeate our raw impressions with intelligence, or what I call the light of the mind, requires the special plasticity and forces of the first three years.[114] We must learn to understand what we see.

The outer light of the Sun that brings the sense world to us must meet a corresponding inner light of mind in order for genuine cognition to occur. In a similar way, if we wish to understand the experiences that arise in meditation, we must find ways to kindle an inner intelligence competent to this new domain of experience. At the outset we are like the French boy who has new experiences but no way to understand them. Yet if we persevere, then, unlike the French boy, we will gradually kindle the new light of mind needed to understand what we experience in meditation. Our task in this chapter and the next will be to develop contemplative practices that support the new thinking we need.

We should be cautious about using understandings and instincts formed in the familiar domain of sense experience to interpret this new realm. These are readily available but likely to be inappropriate for the realm of experience opened up to us through meditation. We should not be surprised by this. The traditional concepts of classical mechanics proved

---

114. For more on this theme see my *Catching the Light* (New York: Oxford University Press, 1993), Chapter 1, or Oliver Sacks' essay "To See and Not See," in *An Anthropologist on Mars* (New York: Knopf, 1995). Brian Friel's touching play *Molly Sweeney* depicts the tragic story of an attempt to recover from blindness.

completely inadequate for the new phenomena of quantum mechanics. Ideas radically different from those of previous science were necessary. New concepts are often required to interpret new phenomena, and this is also true for meditative experience.

In everyday life we know that brilliance in one area of life does not guarantee comparable understanding in another. Not every literature professor can drive a nail, nor is every mathematical genius equally talented in the social arts. Ever since the Harvard psychologist Howard Gardner began to write of multiple intelligences, we have come to realize that some of our most important cognitive capacities can't be captured by a single measure. If we hope to become intelligent meditators, that is to say, if we wish to understand what we experience in meditation, then we need to shape a new intelligence to that end. The remainder of this chapter sketches the means by which this can be done. We will make use of philosophy, mathematics, and further meditative exercises as preparation and practice for that new intelligence.

Aspiring to Insight

Whether at the hand of nature or poetry, our first meditative experiences are like those of the blind French boy who was suddenly given sight. Recall Emerson's sudden flood of unexpected and unfamiliar experiences on the Boston Common. In comparison to his, our initial experiences may be delicate, transient, and elusive. However they begin, over time the territory of meditative experience becomes increasingly familiar to us. Its character becomes richer, our dreams change, and life itself seems to gain other dimensions. In order to discover authentic meaning in these experiences of the inner life, our thinking must become free and mobile in ways that are quite unfamiliar to us. For this reason it is extremely difficult to capture in thought and give expression in words to that which is within. Thoreau wrote, "We may easily multiply the forms of the outward; but to give the within outwardness, that is not easy."[115] In his journals Thoreau struggled daily to capture in words what he had

---

115. Thoreau, in *The Writings of Henry David Thoreau: Journal 1: 1837–1846*, ed. Bradford Torrey (Boston: Houghton Mifflin and Co., 1906), Feb. 3, 1841, p. 189.

experienced so powerfully while tramping through field and swamp. He knew how to multiply the inward experiences of soul that he so prized, but to write them down required so much more. In every meditative moment, we meet the temptation to interpret what we experience with conventional logic and clichéd concepts, according to what Simone Weil calls the "laws of gravity." Deep meditative experience, however, defies the laws of gravity and appears under the sign of grace. Only thinking that is free of the logic of gravity, and is itself graceful, can follow the movements of meditation.

Giving the "within outwardness" requires some measure of understanding. It requires the joining of intelligence to impression, and concept to percept. Every new discovery, scientific or artistic, must undergo this struggle from mere data to intelligibility, and finally achieve expression. A special difficulty arises, however, in the case of meditative experience, because a distinct and novel intelligence is required. To bring the light of intelligence into our meditative experience is to cultivate a spiritual discernment that leads to insight.[116]

The preparation and practices I have described in previous chapters bring health to the soul and clarity to the mind, but the ultimate purpose of meditative schooling is to reach beyond these to the attainment of insights of a type denied to research based exclusively on the physical senses. For many if not most of those who practice meditation today, the explicit aspiration to wisdom is not central to their practice. They seek and are satisfied with the mental and physical benefits that meditation gives, and may never have considered the possibility of research using meditative methods. This should not be construed as criticism of the personal help meditation offers. Society can only be grateful if contemplative practices help to control destructive emotions, or if our scattered attention becomes more focused and sustained. Contemplative movement harmonizes the body, while meditation, properly practiced, balances the mind and mitigates mental suffering. These are welcomed aids to a needy world. From mindfulness to emotional intelligence, the value of various

---

116. Although Howard Gardner may be reluctant to do so, spiritual intelligence should be added to his theory of multiple intelligences. Howard Gardner, *Intelligence Reframed. Multiple intelligences for the 21st century* (New York: Basic Books. 1999), p. 59.

contemplative practices is slowly being confirmed by conventional science with the consequence that such practices are increasingly accepted around the world, independent of the spiritual traditions that originally spawned them. Nevertheless, the true goal of meditation is to achieve a way of directly experiencing the world and ourselves that is not imprisoned or distorted by mental habits and emotional desires. When free of these, we are opened to a richer exploration of reality that presents to us new insights into self and world.

William James was entirely correct in emphasizing the enormous importance of joining empiricism and religion. Science labors under artificial constraints, but Western religion too is unnecessarily shy about the place of meditative experience. The West has had its share of hermits and prophets, but they have been relegated to history and the margins of religious life. Why are we not all encouraged to meditate and aspire to a direct relationship with the divine? As I have already emphasized, Emerson's lament and emphatic call was correct.[117]

> The foregoing generations beheld God and nature face to face; we, through their eyes. Why should not we also enjoy an original relation to the universe? Why should not we have a poetry and philosophy of insight and not of tradition, and a religion by revelation to us, and not the history of theirs?

We all should forge an original and personal relationship to the divine, one that can yield "a poetry and philosophy of insight." We do not do this for self-improvement, but because our age asks it of us. When we think, feel, and act from a place of grace, we are more creative, alive, insightful, and loving.

The motive for seeking spiritual knowledge is not idle curiosity but compassion. The proper means for mitigating suffering and collaborating in the true development of humanity must be grounded in an adequate knowledge of human nature and its full multidimensional character. Good intentions and partial knowledge will not do. Well-intended individuals can cause great harm if they are acting on the basis of a limited

---

117. Ralph Waldo Emerson, *Nature* (1836).

understanding of reality. No one sets out to educate our children poorly, but the results of educational innovation and well-intended pedagogical reforms are unimpressive. Why? Because the understanding of the growing child is too narrow, too impoverished. Half of the child's being, the most important part, namely his or her essential soul-spiritual nature, is left out of account. The reason this aspect of the human being is ignored is not hard to see: the research methods of the academy neglect contemplative inquiry. Using the conventional methods of social science, only material and behavioral factors are observable, and the essential dimensions of the child's nature that are inaccessible to such conventional ways of study are left aside or remain unnoticed.

Every significant problem we confront, whether as individuals or as a civilization, we face blind to half of reality. Health issues, environmental problems, social conflicts, and economic studies all leave out the essential soul-spiritual factors pertinent to each. No wonder our solutions seem to work only half the time. We desperately need to extend the sciences to include disciplined contemplative inquiry. This is what spiritual knowledge means with respect to the human being; we discover the subtle, immaterial dimensions of the world and human nature in detail through the path of meditative inquiry. Then the sciences of economics, government, environment, business, and medicine, as well as the arts, can all be extended fruitfully to include the spiritual. This requires us to embrace the fuller and therefore more adequate conception of the world available through contemplative inquiry and knowing.

As a scientist for my entire adult life, I have prized the certainty of mathematics and physics. I delight in their clarity and power. Early on I also recognized that every field of human investigation can and should be extended in the way described above. It requires no compromise. We can and should make use of all our human capacities for discovery, not limit ourselves to the physical senses alone and to the thinking based on them. We need to cultivate not only a rich, disciplined meditative life, but also the means to illuminate it with understanding. If we do so, our experiences within this arena can become the basis for profound insights, born of a new intelligence, that include the soul-spiritual dimensions of life as well as the material and behavioral aspects. The problems we now confront require this of us more than ever before. The ninth-century Buddhist teacher Shantideva was right when he wrote, "This entire preparation the Sage [Buddha] taught for the sake of wisdom. Thus one wishing to bring an end to suffering should develop wisdom."[118] We need more than material mastery of the outer world; we require an inner knowledge and spiritual mastery as well. Only then will the social and environmental challenges we confront today find an adequate response; only then will we possess the wisdom that will enable us to truly reduce suffering.

The fruits of contemplative inquiry concern innovations not only in practical fields that serve us, but in the creative arts as well. Indeed, all of life is enriched by the new depths of experience that open up in us. Quite literally, we become more fully human—a worthy aspiration and sufficient reason to undertake the long journey of personal development through practice.

Beyond Objects

As we seek a way of knowing suited to meditative experience, we discover that special demands are made on us. Galileo, Newton, and other scientists sought to explain and predict the behavior of objects in the sense world: planets, stones, and machines. Scientists attend to such objects, investigating their behavior in the lab and, through their representations, in theory. Over centuries we have learned the forms of thought perfectly adapted to the inanimate universe. In order to understand the world that opens up to us through meditation, we need to develop forms of thinking that are not focused on inanimate objects, or on any object *per se.* We need our contemplative experiences to grow increasingly free of sense experience. Experience is normally sensual or sense-derived (memories, for example); in meditation, however, this can and should change. Our first contemplative experiences likely have sensual characteristics (colors, sounds, light, warmth, shapes…), but over time such experiences can grow less and less connected to the familiar phenomena of the senses.

When contemplative experiences first appear, one should allow them their own domain of free expression. As I have emphasized before, don't

118. Shantideva, *The Bodhicaryavatara or Guide to the Bodhisattva Way of Life*, trans. Padmakara Translation Group (Boulder, CO: Shambala, 2006) Chapter 9.

try to understand them. The reason for this precaution is that up until this point our thinking has concerned itself chiefly with the phenomena of everyday life. Since we are not accustomed to the phenomena of meditation, we automatically bring to meditative phenomena the conventional logic of normal life. When, in a dream, we try to run and find ourselves moving more and more slowly, we can't understand what is wrong. Another logic is at work in dream-life, one that has its own laws. So too for meditative experience, another kind of thinking is required, and it must be patiently developed before we can hope to comprehend fully the world opening up to us.

We are generally unaware of the ruts in which our thinking runs, but even a little reflection shows that it is largely automatic and associative. The phone rings, we jump up and say, "Hello." Depending on who is on the other end of the phone line, memories stream into our minds without our intending them. A momentary impression stimulates an associated thought or mental image. In speaking we often fall back on clichés and stock responses, strung together with what we have heard others say on the subject, and so on. This kind of thinking is anything but free, and unsuitable to the soul-spiritual realities we will meet in meditation. Associative and automatic thinking force new experiences into old boxes, and so do violence to the novel contemplative domain we are exploring. Truly free thinking that is fully under our conscious control is, to begin with, a special and rare kind of spiritual activity whose character and cultivation I will focus on for the remainder of the chapter.

If in contemplative cognition we are not concerned primarily with objects, with what are we concerned? Briefly stated, instead of a science of objects and their behaviors, the emphasis at this stage of contemplative research is on *relationships, metamorphosis,* and what I will term *agency.* In order to succeed at this new science of spiritual experience we will need to rid ourselves of automatic thinking, which is the habit of reductionism, and learn to think in terms of relationships instead of objects, metamorphosis instead of stasis, and agency instead of mechanism. The example of music can be a help in understanding the roles these three play.

As a composer I set down a tune or melody and its associated harmonies. Music is, in the preceding language, a set of relationships arranged both simultaneously and through time. It may appear as a set of ink spots on paper, but these merely represent a changing set of complex tonal relationships. The tonal relationships morph as quickly as they emerge. I am both the agent of their creation and, as pianist, the agent for their animation. Agency is the activity that creates and maintains the life of the musical piece. We know ourselves as agents, but we can come to appreciate that we are not the only source of agency in the universe. Everything around us springs from agency, which organizes relationships that change over time. At this stage in contemplative practice, we work with form and change, relationships and metamorphosis, and seek to intuit through the changing relationships the spiritual activity or agency in the music we are hearing, the flowering rose, or the dying elm tree.

We face a daunting two-part challenge: first to free ourselves of deeply ingrained habits of mechanistic and materialistic thinking, and second to gradually discover and practice the new ways of thinking suited to the contemplative experience of relationship, metamorphosis, and agency. I wish to emphasize that nothing is wrong with mechanistic and materialistic thinking when applied to the material world. My car is perfectly described by such thinking (although sometimes it seems to have a mind of its own). Even my own physical body is, in part, amenable to mechanistic analysis, although a significant portion of my nature defies that limited logic. If the tiny atom can defy mechanism, why can't I? We are confronting a profound challenge: how to give our full attention to that part of reality that stands at the greatest remove from mechanism. At the outset, we are best advised to free ourselves of that mode of thinking entirely. At a later stage we can reconnect the two modalities as needed.

In order to accomplish this two-part undertaking, we proceed in small steps, each designed to limber up our thinking and to dematerialize it bit by bit. The first step is into the ethereal regions of elementary geometry viewed from a contemplative standpoint.

Halfway to Heaven

For many students, their first encounter with mathematics was fraught with frustration grounded in fear. For others, mathematics became a token for transcendent realities and a certainty unknown in normal life. In the worldview of Pythagoras and Plato, mathematics occupied a position halfway to the pure realm of forms; we might say halfway to heaven. Its purity entranced them and became an essential part of the spiritual discipline expected of their students. Over the door to Plato's Academy were engraved the words, "Let no one unversed in geometry enter here." In his view, through the study of mathematics one accustomed oneself to a life of mind that was at once lucid, and disciplined, and largely free of the senses and distractions of the body. Therefore, Plato reasoned, if we desired to discover the principles that order and form material existence, we should concern ourselves with the immaterial realm of mathematics and philosophy. The statesman as much as the scholar benefited, in Plato's view, from the practice of mathematics. No proper philosopher-king could be unversed in geometry. After all, if Plutarch can be trusted, "Plato said that God geometrized continually."[119] It is only fitting that the philosopher-king should know the workings of God's mind. Of course not everything can be reduced to measurement and mathematics, but even today mathematical exercises can offer us assistance, especially as we attempt to develop a form of thinking sufficiently free and fluid to comprehend the pure relationships that arise in contemplative inquiry.

One of the simplest geometric relationships is expressed in the triangle. We can use it to explore the triad of relationship, metamorphosis, and agency. The triangle is commonly defined as a geometrical figure whose three sides are formed by straight lines lying in a plane. We can begin by considering the triangle drawn below. Is it a triangle, really? Are the lines that make up its sides perfectly straight, or infinitely long and thin? True lines must be so, but the drawn lines cannot embody such ideal characteristics. Obviously, a drawn triangle is more of a symbol for the ideal mental picture of three perfect lines lying in a single plane, intersecting in three points. Use the drawn image to help you imagine a true triangle. A very particular relationship is expressed in the triangle, which distinguishes it from a circle, square, or any other form. Mathematics is, one could say, all about pure relationships. Everything extraneous is taken away. It is absurd to think of a "roundish" or "squareish" triangle. It would be no triangle at all. Triangles possess their own nature, pure and simple.

---

119. Plutarch, *Convivialium disputationum*, liber 8,2.

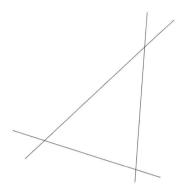

Once you have a triangle in mind, allow it to change. For example, move one of the triangle's sides, keeping the others fixed, as in the figures *a* and *b* below. As long as the line remains in the plane formed by the other two, you always end up with a triangle again, although different in details from the original. After playing with one side, allow a second side to shift and keep only a single line fixed. Take your time, simultaneously allowing the two sides to move freely in the plane to the left or right, pivoting as they move. Finally permit the third side to shift and pivot as well so that all three are moving. In your mind's eye, you can continue to change the placement of the three sides. No matter what the change, in every instance, you still have triangles, or a triangle in metamorphosis. The triangle's size and angles change, but its nature as a triangle remains. Spend time shifting and pivoting the sides of the triangles; feel yourself in the continuous transformation, while attending also to the whole formed of the three lines and their relationship. This is the experience of metamorphosis. Although the particular shape changes, the triangle relationship persists throughout.

Finally ask yourself, what is it that allows me to recognize in the infinite variety of particular forms that each is a triangle? With this question we reach beyond the particular toward the general. The mental image of a metamorphosing triangle disappears. We look for something that is common to all individual instances of triangle, something that is embodied in the particular but is nothing particular itself. In this way we reach toward and intuit the idea or pure concept: triangle. Notice that the concept triangle doesn't "look" like a triangle. It doesn't look like anything, because we are now at the level of pure thought.

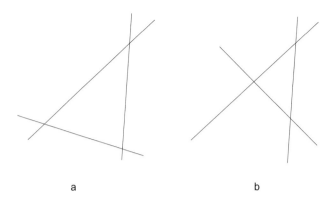

a   b

In this exercise we have moved from a crude sense image (a symbol of a triangle) to a static mental image, to a triangular image in movement, and finally through the flux of individual triangles we leap to the pure thought: triangle. The sequence is archetypal. In the language I introduced earlier, the mental image embodies the pure relationship "triangle." By bringing it into movement we free ourselves from the habit of seeing "triangle" as something particular. In order to determine what all the individual instances have in common; we must reach even beyond triangles in motion to the pure thought: triangle. The thought "triangle" is not dead or fixed, but generative. Thinking and feeling our way into the exercise we realize that the idea of the triangle is the "agent." In this way, little by little, we come to appreciate the living, creative power of the thought world. As a realm of agency, it is quite different from the dead, abstract thought-world we normally associate with thought.

Through exercises such as this, which is based on one given by Rudolf Steiner,[120] we become aware of the real spiritual activity that is at once active in us and in the world, and which we call thinking. We learn to live in movement while simultaneously recognizing the element of form: metamorphosis and enduring relationship. From the atmosphere around us to the galaxies above us, the universe is ceaselessly changing, but within it are enduring principles or truths. Pythagoras saw number or

---

120. Rudolf Steiner, *Human and Cosmic Thought*, trans. Charles Davy (London: Rudolf Steiner Press, nd) pp. 9–14.

pure relationship as the architectonic principle that formed all existence. Kepler echoed this sentiment when he declared, "Geometry, which before the origin of things was coeternal with the divine mind, supplied God with patterns for the creation of the world, and passed over to Man along with the image of God."[121] The poet and mathematician Novalis notes, "True mathematics is the proper element of the Magi. The life of the gods is mathematics. Pure mathematics is religion."[122]

At a certain stage of contemplative experience, movement and metamorphosis are a key feature. We are beyond the object triangle as static image, and we live instead in a realm of metamorphosis that is both free and constrained. Three lines shift and turn (metamorphose) with the single constraint that they lie in a plane, and that alone is enough to insure the relationship: "triangleness." We can build on the simple geometric exercise above in a way that will help us to develop a capacity for insight in the midst of change. Through the study of mathematical transformation, we not only discover the hidden beauty and harmony of geometry, but also can learn to see its expression in nature and ourselves. We come to notice constancy and lawfulness in the midst of ceaseless movement and metamorphosis. Exactly this capacity for seeing constant relationships in the flux of experience is required for our contemplative life, and especially for contemplative knowing.

Geometry as Transformation

The formulation of geometry developed by Euclid (c.300 B.C.E.) dominated mathematics until the nineteenth century. Kant even raised Euclidean geometry to the rarified status of a truth concerning space that required no empirical justification. Only during the nineteenth century did mathematicians like Bolyai, Lobachevsky, Riemann, and Gauss successfully challenge Euclid's "self-evident" axioms and postulates. With the liberation of the mathematical imagination from the rigid Euclidean

---

121. Johannes Kepler, *The Harmony of the World* (Linz , 1619), Book IV, Ch. 1. Trans. E. J. Aiton, A. M. Duncan, and J. V. Field (1997), p. 304.

122. Arthur Zajonc, "An Aeolian Harp: Nature and Novalis' Science," *Journal for Anthroposophy,* Number 32, Autumn 1980, p. 70.

mindset, a raft of novel non-Euclidean geometries was quickly developed. No longer was a single geometry *a priori* true. Many could and did claim equal standing. If one was concerned to know the geometry of real physical space, then, contrary to Kant's claim, one had to determine it through measurement. This was first attempted by Gauss (unsuccessfully), but such measurements continue today. For example, astrophysicists have successfully used observations of microwave background radiation to determine the large-scale geometry of the universe, and Einstein's General Theory of Relativity made full use of a non-Euclidean, curved space-time.

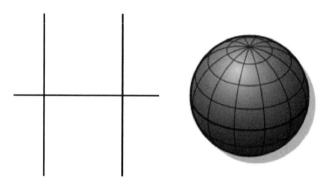

In the new non-Euclidean geometries old ideas, like that of the triangle, take on a new meaning. For example, in the case of geometry on a sphere, the shape of the triangle changes. If we lay three lines on a sphere, strange things happen. Consider the earth. Let one line be the equator, and let the two others be great circles (i.e. lines of longitude). The two great circles meet the equator in a right angle. Think about the same construction on a plane. If the two lines meet a third at right angles then the two lines would be parallel and never meet. On a sphere they meet at the north and south poles! Through this single example, we can begin to appreciate how fluid the new geometries of curved space are. We are challenged to break with the rigid forms of traditional Euclidean geometry and to adopt a more flexible mindset. Yet the multiplication of geometries seems profligate and confusing.

Suddenly nineteenth-century mathematicians were beset with the embarrassment of multiple geometries; how could one classify them? What deep organizing principles could bring order to the proliferation within geometrical thinking? In 1872 the German mathematician Felix Klein advanced his so-called Erlangen program, named after the university town in which he taught. It organized geometries according to their transformational properties; more specifically, according to those properties that remained constant in the midst of change. As contemplative practitioners, the Erlangen program helps us to understand how we can find our bearings in a universe of shifting forms. At a certain stage, meditative experience takes on the character of fluid change, the loss of the familiar, and we need to practice discovering constancy in change. Transformation in geometry offers a clear exemplar.

Consider the simplest transformations: translation and rotation. The triangle on the left is translated to the right and rotated. Notice that under translation and rotation the interior angles of the triangles and the lengths of the sides are unchanged. These properties are said to be "invariant" under translation and rotation (which are called orthogonal transformations).

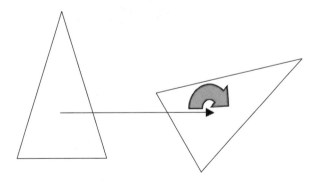

Pick up a book and move it through space. All the motions you can perform with the book are merely a combination of translations and rotations. In fact, this is true for any and all rigid bodies: your car, your phone, the coins in your pocket. The only kinds of motion they can make are rotations and translation. But not all objects of our world are rigid. Tip over a glass of water. The same volume of water is now on the floor but the shape of the water is totally different from the shape it had in the glass. Dust a pan of water with powder and pull your finger through the water. The sequence of vortices looks like the figure below. A plant leaf may have a similar form throughout its growth, but the leaf expands. Clearly, the rigid transformations of rotation and translation are insufficient to capture the full range of change we see, much less that which appears in our contemplative experience.

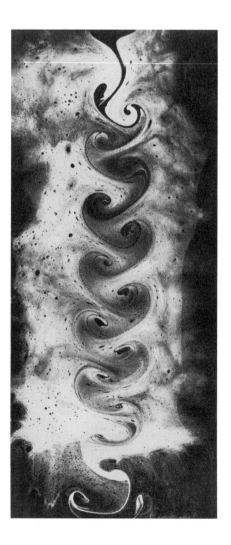

As a second example we begin with the same triangle but now in addition permit a change of scale (similarity transformation). The shaded triangle is smaller, so the sides are no longer the same as they were originally; that is, their lengths are not invariant under a similarity transformation.

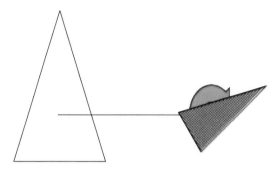

The living world is full of such transformations. A leaf displays a shape that stays largely the same but whose size changes. In the figure below, the size of the leaf increases, but clearly other processes are at work that change its shape as well.[123] We will return to these later.

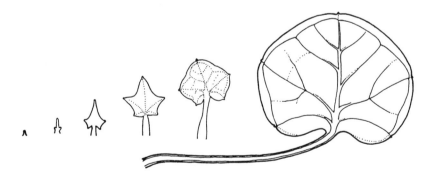

123. Jochen Bockemühl, ed. *Erscheinungsformen des Ätherischen* (Stuttgart: Verlag Freies Geistesleben, 1977) p. 116.

The concepts of transformation and invariance are crucial to understanding the Erlangen program. Rigid adherence to Euclidian thinking was broken during the nineteenth century, but almost immediately a new way of orienting oneself, of finding order in the apparent chaos of geometries, was discovered. The features that remain invariant under transformations of different types can be used to classify the different geometries. This idea proved invaluable when Einstein made the final break with classical physics in his special and general theories of relativity. Here again old invariances such as length and temporal duration were cast aside, but immediately new and more subtle invariances emerged.[124] Important parallels exist between the challenges faced by Einstein and what we face in making sense of our meditative experiences. Much of our old thinking will need to be cast aside, but new spiritual truths will show themselves to the new enlivened thinking we develop through such exercises as these. Fortunately, we needn't be an Einstein to make the changes to thinking required to gain contemplative insights.

In the above examples, though we have increased our range of movement incrementally, we have obviously been working under severe constraints. Projective geometry offers us the greatest flexibility possible, with the single constraint that straight lines transform to straight lines. Angles, lengths, and certain other properties of the triangle can vary, but straight lines will transform into straight lines no matter what. Triangles remain triangles but can change size and shape and even tolerate sending one or more vertices to infinity! Projective transformations get their name because the method for constructing them makes use of projection and section.[125] In the figure below, the point O is the center of projection. The points X',Y', and Z' are mapped to the points X",Y", and Z", which form two triangles (darker lines). One sees that the pairs of points are related by a projection by the three lines through O that also go through the pairs of points. The diagram also shows a remarkable feature of the two triangles: corresponding sides, when extended, meet in points that all lie on a single line o. This is always true of triangles related by a

124. The space-time interval is an invariant under the Lorentz transformations of special relativity.

125. Olive Whicher, *Projective Geometry*, (London: Rudolf Steiner Press, 1971), p. 172.

projective transformation. We see that, as great as the freedom is under projective transformations, order can still be found in subtle and sometimes hidden ways. This is a crucial lesson for our new thinking. It will live in a fluid element with a similar subtle order.

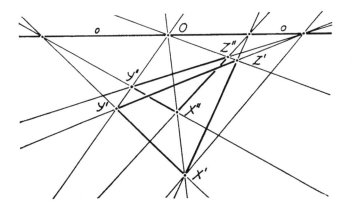

The liberation experienced in the pristine realm of geometry has taken place in other fields as well. Think of the developments in late nineteenth-century art (the Impressionists Pissarro, Manet, and Cézanne, for example) that presaged the complete revolution shown in the work of Kandinsky and Picasso. Kandinsky longed for "the spiritual in art," which required him to throw off the last vestiges of representational art in order to free his imagination to express the intangible promptings and perceptions of spirit. Like him, if we would "think the spiritual," then we need to free ourselves from the rigid limitations of a Euclidean mentality and develop a far more plastic and mobile way of understanding. Inwardly we can learn to translate, rotate, grow, and transform our thinking. The challenge in these geometrical exercises (and they are challenging!) is to follow inwardly the stages of outer construction. It is essential to move the changes in line and figure in imagination and not only follow them on the paper. In doing so, we are not trading Euclidean security for pure chaos. Subtle order still prevails. Invariant features remain, acting like the Pole star in the night sky, unmoving while others move around it. We can navigate by Polaris even if all the familiar features of the shoreline have receded from view and we are tossed on an unknown sea. In this way certain kinds of mathematical exercises can be enormously helpful in freeing our thinking while allowing us to maintain clarity and precision throughout. This is exactly the kind of new thinking we will need in order to understand what we experience in meditation: flexible yet sensitive to a new and subtle order.

Peripheral Thinking

Another mathematical exercise will help to unfetter us from a particular convention of thinking that is deepseated in many of us. When my fellow scientists and I consider the material objects around us, we automatically think of them in terms of atoms. We build up reality point by point, atom by atom. Similarly, we involuntarily think of geometric forms as built up point by point. For example, the common definition of a circle is: "all points equidistant from a given point." The upper figure to the right shows a set of concentric circles comprised of points. It is easy to imagine many more points filling in the spaces to form other circles built up point by point. Call them "point-wise circles." The mechanical device of a compass draws all points that are the same distance from a given point, the center.

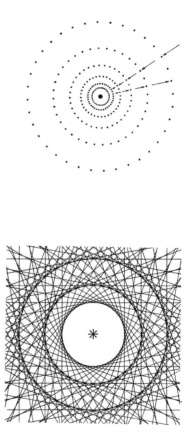

Another equally valid way of thinking about circles, however, is from the outside or periphery. Working this way strengthens what I call peripheral thinking. The figure below the point-wise circles is a set of three "line-wise" circles. These are formed by the set of lines (not points) that are tangent to the three circles. The lines embrace the three circles, which are easily seen within them.

Think of the way a sculptor or potter fashions her work. The clay is shaped by her hands pressing from the outside. In an analogous way, the line-wise circles are surrounded as if by an infinity of open hands, each of whose palm delicately touches the surface at one point. A circle can be created by a sheaf of tangent lines as well as by a set of equidistant points; both have comparable mathematical precision and rigor.

One crucial, if challenging, geometrical exercise remains to be done. All the transformations we have considered so far, such as moving the sides of a triangle, or even the projective transformation of one triangle to another, have moved points to points or lines to lines. Our thinking needs one further liberation. When we imagine transformations that change points to lines and lines to points, we unify the two ways of drawing circles (point-wise and line-wise). Transformations that change points to lines are especially beautiful and of great significance as we cross from an atomistic consciousness to a holistic one. We will need to make exactly this transition in thinking in order to bring the light of understanding to our holistic world of spiritual experience. The mathematical transformation we will now perform is a precise metaphor for the transformation toward holistic thinking that spiritual understanding requires.

We begin with a circle on the page. It divides the page into two parts: the part inside the circle and the part outside. Select a single point "**a**" on the outside and draw two lines through the point that just touch the circle—i.e., that are tangent to it. Only two such lines exist, and each touches the circle in one point. Now draw a line, defined by the two tangent points, that intersects the circle. This line, labeled "**A**," is the line *in correspondence* to the outer point labeled "**a**."

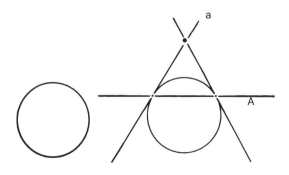

The same construction can be used to find the lines through the circle that correspond to any number of points outside it. In the figure drawn below, I happen to have chosen points that are all equidistant from the center of the circle. In drawing the corresponding lines within the circle, I have left out the intermediate construction lines for all of them but one.

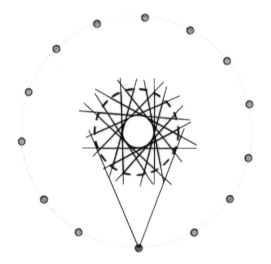

Since the outside points lie on a circle, the lines corresponding to them create a corresponding inner circle. Note that the inner circle is not defined by a set of points but rather by a family of lines that embrace it. In this way we are able to bring the point-wise outer circle into an exact correspondence with a line-wise inner circle. Form is related to form through a transformation that changes points to lines. The figure below shows the complementary construction: a set of interior points is placed into correspondence with a set of exterior lines.[126] If one were to think of the region inside the circle as "space" then the region outside the circle could be thought of as a "counterspace." Space and counterspace stand in a beautiful geometric correspondence. We need to learn to think and live our way into both as we seek to join thinking to inner experience.

---

126. Ibid., p. 201.

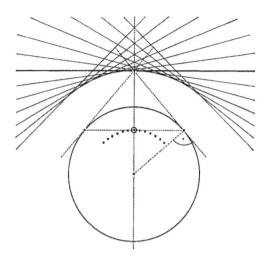

The next time you see something or meet someone, don't think of them as built of parts from the inside but rather as sculpted as a whole from the periphery. The sensation is a bit like someone suggesting that you become aware of the space behind you—your "backspace." We are so intent on looking forward that we forget the backspace. Likewise, we are so intent on points that we neglect the periphery. This is a pity, because the periphery is the place of spontaneity, creativity, and the unexpected. The Soviets had a centrally planned economy, but Western-style economies are planned by no one. Western political campaigns have planning headquarters, but Socrates, Buddha, and Jesus all seemed to wander through their respective cities and countrysides spontaneously responding to those they encountered. They taught, healed the lame, and fed the hungry without the advantage of a large staff or a strategic plan. The lesson I take from this fact is that if, like an improv artist, one can creatively respond to what emerges from the periphery, truly enduring consequences follow. We would benefit from much less central planning and far more peripheral planning.

Of Wholes and Parts

When you hear the word "interconnectedness," what do you think of? Each of us has a circle of friends and acquaintances. We are related to each of them and they to us. Likewise, when we consider the objects of the world, we think of each as related to a set of others. As the number increases we appreciate the quantitative increase of interconnections but generally fail to recognize any qualitative change. The point-wise picture of relationships just described has profound limitations not only theoretically but in everyday life. Perhaps you have had the following experience. An elder in your care adds a single new medicine and everything goes haywire. According to the standard analysis of the pharmacist, the new medicine should not conflict with any of the other medicines considered individually. The false premise is that medicines only work one on one. In fact, a set of medicines become a biochemical whole with which the new medicine interacts. One can no longer think in terms of pairs of interactions between individual medicines. The biochemical whole possesses its own full reality, which is not reducible to simple pair-wise relationships.

A second example is the phenomenon of human interactions in institutional settings. Your individual interactions with each person in your work environment can be very different from, indeed contrary to, your experience of the same people in a meeting. Situate the officemates in the board conference room with everyone else in the department, and they suddenly become entirely different people. The whole setting conditions everyone's interactions and any attempt to assign blame or power to one individual is misguided. The well-known organizational expert Peter Senge has written extensively on such organic relationships in businesses. If you are unaware of this alternative principle of organization, you will likely be confused and ineffective as a business leader. Again we easily fall into the fallacy of pair-wise analysis and forget the often overwhelming power of the whole. The whole is its own beast or angel, and we are better off not thinking of it in terms of parts at all. Its attributes emerge from the coalescence of many contributing factors but usually bear no direct resemblance to any one of them.

The previous geometrical exercise can help us break out of the pairwise, point-to-point mentality that tyrannizes our normal thinking. In the exercise, you will have noticed that the transformation was from point to line. I arranged a set of points to form a circle, and a corresponding set of lines emerged that encompassed a new circle. The construction (called a "pole-polar" transformation) can do its magic on any shape, pairing any set of points outside the circle with a sheaf of lines inside. This particular feature can help us to understand holistic, organic organization in the world.

Kant, Goethe, Steiner, Hans Jonas, and others have sought a distinct type of organizational principle suited to the organic.[127] I think the relationship they sought between wholes and parts is analogous to the pole-polar transformation. They sought a means of relating every part of the organism to all others. In the pole-polar transformation we have an example in which a whole line can be transformed into a single point. We can find another analogy in the ancient Hermetic tradition, in which authors frequently wrote of the macrocosm being reflected in the microcosm. In Indian mythology Indra's net is comprised of countless jewels in each one of which all the other jewels find their reflection. All these are images of holistic interconnections, a many-to-one map or transformation. Relationships are not only direct, or even complex; they are sometimes holistic. Through meditation we cross a threshold into the realm of Indra's net, into holistic relationships, and we will need a many-to-one mode of consciousness if we are to make our way.

Quantum Holism

Before leaving the topic of geometry and movement, I must point to an important related development in quantum mechanics, particularly as worked out by David Bohm. He advocated for a new mentality needed to work with the new physics.[128] Many of the lessons Bohm took from quantum physics are immediately applicable to the holistic relationships that are part of contemplative experience.

Holism has gradually become accepted as a central feature of quantum mechanics, and Bohm's understanding of quantum physics reflects this view with particular clarity. The conventional physics of discrete objects so familiar to us from daily life—the "explicate order," as Bohm called

---

127. Hans Jonas, *The Phenomenon of Life: Toward a Philosophical Biology* (Evanston, IL: Northwestern University Press, 2001). Steiner wrote, for example in *Theosophy*, of a distinct immaterial "etheric" aspect to the life world. It is organized according to holistic relationships, constant metamorphosis, and an openness to higher agency.
128. David Bohm, *Wholeness and the Implicate Order* (London: Routledge, 2002).

it—cannot be used to account for quantum phenomena. The experimental facts of quantum mechanics demand a holism or "implicate order" that defies our conventional notion of reality as comprised of separate objects, each with an unambiguous set of identifying attributes.

An analogy often used by Bohm to characterize the implicate order is that of the hologram. A hologram is made by splitting a beam of laser light into two parts. One part falls directly on a film plate while the second part illuminates the object of interest. The laser light that is scattered from the object also falls on the film plate, and the interference between the two kinds of light (direct and scattered) is recorded on the film. When developed, the film displays not an image of the object, but a maze of tiny light and dark regions. However, when laser light passes through the film, a reconstructed three-dimensional image hangs in space before us. The magic of the hologram lies in the special type of transformation involved. Like the transformation of a whole line into a single point described earlier, in the hologram the whole object is projected onto every point of the film. Instead of the one-to-one, point-wise projection common to normal photographs, the hologram images the whole object to every point. Cut the film in half, and a laser light will still render the whole image visible.[129] Quantum mechanics embodies an analogous holism, and one that is non-classical in crucial ways. The name given by Schrödinger to this feature of quantum mechanics is *entanglement*.

When you set the table for dinner the knife goes to the left of the spoon, but the spatial arrangement is determined merely by cultural convention. The order could be reversed with no real consequences. This is not the case for the pair of numbers 21. Reverse them and you get 12, which has a different meaning altogether because 21 and 12 each must be read as a whole. Reading the words on this page is also evidence for the importance of order and wholes. The order of some juxtaposed objects can be reversed with impunity, but not so with others that form wholes. In quantum mechanics the holism goes much deeper. In it we

---

129. When cut in half, the resulting image is slightly degraded in resolution but not in size. The theory of holography encompasses only classical optics and the mathematics of the holistic Fourier transform, so we do not need quantum mechanics to account for the characteristics of the hologram, but it is a helpful analogy.

are no longer dealing with spoons and knives but with exotic elementary particles. When we juxtapose two of them their individual identity is called into question. We still see the 1 and the 2 in 21. Not so with juxtaposed elementary particles. In most cases they lose their individual identity and become a new and conceptually indivisible entity. This is sometimes termed "ontological emergence," which is to say the identity of parts recedes and *real* holism arises.[130]

To see how this works requires only a bit of algebra. The wave function is the mathematical entity that represents the quantum system under study. If the system is composed of two *independent* particles then the wave function for the two-particle system Ψ is simply the product of the wave function for each particle separately, φ_a and φ_b. For the whole system, the wave function is therefore given by:

$$\Psi = \varphi_a \varphi_b$$

If the two particles are not completely independent, but interact in some way, which is usually the case, then a new possibility arises. The two particles can be exchanged. If the exchange produces a result that, to the experimenter, is indistinguishable from the original situation, then a completely new kind of quantum state is produced called an "entangled" state, notated by the expression:

$$\Psi = \varphi_a \varphi_b + \varphi_b \varphi_a$$

This state cannot be broken up (i.e., it cannot be mathematically "factorized") into the product of wave functions for two separate particles. This means we can no longer think of the system as comprised of two well-defined individual particles. The attributes of each particle become "non-local," and new experimental features appear for such entangled systems. The experimental consequences of the new state are unambiguous indications that something profoundly new exists, unlike any classical physical system. No longer can we ascribe distinct identifying properties

---

130. Michael Silberstein and John McGeever, "The Search for Ontological Emergence," *The Philosophical Quarterly*, vol. 49, April 1999, pp. 182–200.

to the particles separately. In a strange sense, the individual particles give up their identifying attributes to the whole. Physicists term this quantum holism, and have used it in order to develop the whole new area of quantum computing.[131] Holism is now a fact of the quantum world. When introducing this chapter I wrote about relationships. Quantum holism is a new kind of relationship.

In addition, quantum mechanics is inherently active. Following Alfred North Whitehead, the physicist David Finkelstein has maintained for years that quantum physics is best understood in terms of processes instead of objects, in terms of verbs instead of nouns.[132] Bohm combines this view with holism and speaks of "holomovement." I take each of these efforts to be a call for a new mentality that is not only required for the science of quantum mechanics, but is also well suited to contemplative inquiry. We need to learn to think in wholes and in movement, that is, in holomovement. This is a requirement not only of quantum mechanics, but also for achieving contemplative insight.

All around us geometry combines with movement. The figure skater glides across the ice (translation), opens her arms wide, extends one leg (expansion), and begins a spin (rotation). As she draws her limbs toward her (contraction), her speed of rotation increases. The dervish whirls round and round (rotation), his right hand opened upward to God, his left hand opened downward to the earth. Like the dervish and the skater, we embody geometry and movement in our motions. We can bring mindfulness into them through the practice of contemplative movement, be it in the form of yoga, eurythmy, or tai chi, but what is outer can also become inner. In playing ring-around-the-rosy, children dance a circle. Only after they have moved in the form of a circle do they draw it, and much later they learn to think of the circle abstractly. Like them we can benefit from mindfully enacting the changes with our bodies in eurythmy or yoga and then imagining them in our mind's eye. Having moved and imagined, we can open out into silent awareness, release

131. George Greenstein and Arthur Zajonc, *The Quantum Challenge*, 2nd ed. (Sudbury, MA: Jones and Bartlett, 2005).

132. Timothy E. Eastman and Hank Keeton, eds., *Physics and Whitehead: Quantum, Process, and Experience* (Albany, NY: SUNY Press, 2003).

the experience of movement, and find our way as usual into pure open attention and the afterimage.

Through mental exercises such as those I have given, we can internalize the transformations common to material bodies (translations, rotations) and begin to add to them the transformations more prevalent in the life world (expansion, contraction, projective and holistic transformations).[133] As we cross the threshold in meditation, we find our bearings by seeking out subtle invariant relationships. In all that changes, what remains unchanged; in metamorphosis, what is the enduring form? The unchanging may be hidden at first, but through such exercises as these we learn to seek and find the pole star of meditative experience.

---

133. Arthur Zajonc, "The Geometry of Life: Towards a Science of Form," *Orion Magazine*, Winter 1985, pp. 48–59.

Chapter Seven

Contemplative Inquiry

One comes to know nothing

beyond what one loves. And the deeper

and more complete the knowledge,

the stronger, more powerful and living

must be one's love and fervor.[134]

— Goethe

We have become increasingly familiar with the stages of contemplation. Contemplative inquiry rests on the sound moral foundations of humility and reverence. In addition, the practitioner cultivates his or her powers of concentrated attention, equanimity in the feeling life, and a strengthened resolve. On this basis, one undertakes meditation as cognitive breathing, selecting a word, image, sense content, or situation for concentrated attention and open awareness. The afterimage or echo that emerges in Simone Weil's "void" reflects a threshold crossing of consciousness. The object of our attention recedes or disappears, and one senses the subtle presence of another reality. In the traditional language of world spirituality, one has crossed the threshold between material reality and that of the spirit.

---

134. Johann Wolfgang von Goethe, *Trost bei Goethe*, ed. Heinrich Tieck, trans. Arthur Zajonc (München: Langen Müller, 1998), p. 69.

At first, our experience after the crossing is colored by the psyche and the trappings of the sense world, but we can also recognize the uniqueness at the heart of these experiences. They are like nothing we have known before. While we sense and seek some meaning in them beyond the "blooming buzzing confusion" of mere sensation described by William James,[135] conventional analysis is inadequate and misleading for our purposes.

As I have emphasized, new experience must be joined with new thinking if new knowledge is to result. New insight requires new concepts as well as new percepts. We require a way of bringing experience and reason together, a way of perceiving meaning in the given, even when the given arises through deep meditation. The qualities of the new thinking we require are developed, for example, by mathematical exercises of the kind we have just completed. Work with pure philosophical thinking can have a similar salutary effect. Mobility in thought, the ability to sustain complexity or even contradiction, and an appreciation for conceptual holism, are features of a new intelligence necessary for contemplative knowing. Here too is the wellspring of originality and creativity. The artist can only see the new, can only truly create from this space of freedom.

Indeed, when Goethe maintained that one can only come to know that which one loves, he had in mind an understanding of knowing that ranged far beyond information processing. Such knowing is not distant from the object to be known, nor is it exploitative. Its motives are high, its methods gentle, and its interests selfless. It is time to articulate and practice an epistemology of love instead of one of separation.

Toward an Epistemology of Love

Every object, well contemplated,

opens a new organ in us.

— GOETHE

---

135. William James, "Percept and Concept—The Import of Concepts," *Some Problems of Philosophy* (Cambridge, MA: Harvard University Press, 1979).

A new intelligence and theory of knowledge are required if we are to transform our meditative experiences into contemplative knowing. What are the characteristics of this new intelligence? Perhaps surprisingly, here we are helped at least as much by the poets as by the philosophers. Novalis recognized that[136]

> The spirit world is in fact revealed to us; it is always open. Could we suddenly become as sensitive as is necessary, we should perceive ourselves to be in its midst. What are the methods for healing our present deficient condition? Formerly they were fasts and moral purification; now maybe invigoration.

The door to Novalis's spirit world is located in consciousness and is locked only from our side. Opening the door requires exactly the invigorating practices of mind and heart that I have been describing.

In his essay "The Poet," Emerson characterized a way of being, knowing, and speaking that connected the human being to "the true circuit of things." According to Emerson, the poet knew by means of a form of insight that he termed Imagination.[137]

> This insight, which expresses itself by what is called Imagination, is a very high sort of seeing, which does not come by study, but by the intellect being where and what it sees, by sharing the path, or circuit of things through forms, and so making them translucid to others. The path of things is silent. Will they suffer a speaker to go with them? A spy they will not suffer; a lover, a poet, is the transcendency of their own nature,—him they will suffer. The condition of true naming, on the poet's part, is his resigning himself to the divine aura which breathes through forms, and accompanying that.

---

136. Novalis, *The Disciples at Saïs and Other Fragments*, trans. F.V.M.T. and U.C.B. (London: Methuen & Co., 1903), p. 79.
137. Ralph Waldo Emerson, "The Poet," in *Emerson's Essays* (New York: Thomas Y. Crowell), pp. 278–79.

Imaginative insight, as described here by Emerson, is not ungrounded fantasy but a way of genuine knowing. His description presents us with some of the main characteristics of that form of intelligence.

The first characteristic of an epistemology of love is what I call *respect* for the intrinsic nature of the other. When we meet someone, whether a new acquaintance or an old friend, we begin by honoring them. Their inherent value and identity is thereby acknowledged. When Rilke writes about love, he advises lovers to "stand guard over the solitude of the other." In saying this, he is advocating a relationship to the beloved that begins with respect for his or her unique identity and infinite potential.[138] What is true regarding those we love is also true regarding any object or being we wish to know better. We begin by recognizing that what is before us possesses inherent value and is worthy of our respect. In Emerson's universe, the poet and not the spy is permitted to travel the full circuit of existence, because he is a lover. Respect is the foundation of contemplative inquiry.

In an aphorism, Goethe once called this way of investigation "a delicate empiricism that makes itself utterly identical with the object, thereby becoming true theory."[139] In these few words we meet several further characteristics of an epistemology of love. The empiricism advocated by Francis Bacon, the great British proponent of the scientific method, was anything but gentle. Instead, one was advised to press nature to extreme states in order to force her secrets from her. *Gentleness*, however, is the second characteristic of the contemplative way of knowing. Goethe's aphorism also asks that we join our own essential nature with the interior dimensions of the world. Thus to respect and gentleness we must add *intimacy* and *participation*. Where normal science distances the observer from the observed by objectifying the latter, an epistemology of love moves toward the subject of study. Indeed, intimacy here implies not only proximity but a participation in the interior dynamic that produces the object. This last thought requires explanation.

---

138. Rilke, *Love and other Difficulties*, ed. and trans. John J. L. Mood (New York: W. W. Norton, 1975), p. 28. Buber also emphasizes this view in *I and Thou*.
139. Goethe, *Scientific Studies*, ed. and trans. Douglas Miller, "Maxims and Reflections," (New York: Suhrkamp Pub., 1988), p. 307.

Too often we view the world around us as if it were a series of still life photographs: static and inert. To see that this view belies reality, consider yourself. When seen from the outside, you appear as a set of relatively static images and behaviors. These are but a poor reflection of the dynamic reality you really are. You are biologically, psychically, and spiritually alive. Like a river, your thoughts, feelings, and volition are in constant motion, streaming ceaselessly, taking new forms and unexpected turns. *Participation* allows us to reach past the static outer images to the inner activity of the other. We learn to move ourselves according to the dynamic reality that is the other. We become one with their living interior.

At first hearing this may sound like a rare mystical state, but we participate in the world of others all the time when we enter into their thoughts and feelings, whether in conversation or through literature. It is really quite miraculous that a complex set of noises or scribbles on a page, which we call syllables and letters, is sufficient for us to communicate. Note too that "communicate" shares a Latin root with "communion," which literally means "to participate." We think the thought of the other in order to understand him or her. In a similar way, we must learn to think the thought that is active within each and every object to which we give our attention. Such participation requires that we resign ourselves to what Emerson calls "the divine aura of things."

Three preconditions must be met in order for us to attain such insight. I call them *vulnerability, transformation,* and *organ formation.* If we simply bring our old self, our habitual ways of seeing and knowing, then little that is truly new can be expected. Therefore, at this point, the strength we must possess shows itself as vulnerability, as a kind of weakness and openness to ambiguity. Rage and fear sever our relations to others such that we can neither see nor hear truly. In order to enter fully and objectively into the thoughts and feelings of the other, we must be vulnerable to them, resign ourselves to them, respectfully, gently, and intimately. Only when we are vulnerable can we become where and what the other is; then we participate in their world. The other flows through us.

Like the river whose bed is formed by the water's movement, we are *transformed* by the flow of living thoughts that animate everything and now pass through us. How does this happen? Goethe tells us when he writes, "Every object well contemplated creates an organ of perception in us."[140] Our physical organ of sight was created in exactly this way: "From among the lesser ancillary organs of the animals, light has called forth one organ to become its like, and thus the eye was formed by the light and for the light so that the inner light may emerge to meet the outer light."[141] The organs we need for insight are fashioned by attention and immersion in the object of contemplation. With every repetition, the cycle of attention and formation is at work fashioning the organs required for contemplative knowing.

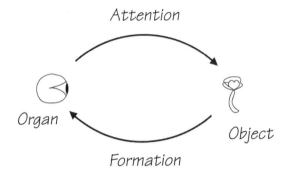

Attention

Organ

Object

Formation

In addition to the organ of cognition, understanding requires the light of intelligence. In ancient Greece, the philosopher Empedocles wrote that the eye is the lantern of the body.[142] Fashioned from the elements by the divine Aphrodite with rivets of love, the eye was thought to have been lit at the fire of creation and to carry within it an "ocular fire." The light from that fire, streaming out through hidden passages in the eye to illuminate the world, in Empedocles' theory gave us our vision. While we no longer believe in a physical light streaming from the eye, the metaphor is still accurate in that the outer light of the Sun must join to the light of the mind for insight to arise. Moreover, the particular form of that light must be suited to the level of experience. In the last chapter,

---

140. Goethe, *Scientific Studies*, "Significant Help Given by an Ingenious Turn of Phrase," p. 39.
141. Goethe, *Scientific Studies*, Preface to "Theory of Color," p. 164.
142. Kathleen Freeman, *Ancilla to the Pre-Socratic Philosophers* (Cambridge, MA: Harvard University Press, 1983), p. 61.

for example, we saw that mechanistic thinking is inadequate for under-standing genuine holistic phenomena. Therefore, to each level of organ formation we must add a specific *illumination*.

The fruit of transformation, organ formation, and illumination is Emerson's "true naming," or Goethe's "true theory." Remember that in ancient Greek the word *theoria* meant "to behold." As Emerson said, insight "is a very high sort of seeing, which does not come by study, but by the intellect being where and what it sees." We seek exactly such see-ing as the way of knowing best suited to meditative investigation.

Knowledge is an event, not an object. We have all struggled through incomprehension to a moment of clear insight in which we "saw" what had so long eluded us. Writing it down, or even describing it to another, may have produced only blank looks if our partner was not ready to see what we had seen. In other words, such epiphanies are always personal, and conveying them is a challenge. Contemplative knowing, likewise, is personal and experiential. Therefore, in order to communicate it fully we must find a way to lead others to the same experience. They too must come to "see" what we have come to know. The very stuff of knowledge is, therefore, insubstantial, and yet it is what the world is built of. Atoms themselves are nothing more than this. When we abandon an outmoded materialist ontology for an "ontology of meaning," the new intelligence is experienced as a high form of seeing, the *aperçu*, so crucial to discov-ery. "In science, however, the treatment is null, and all efficacy lies in the *aperçu*," wrote Goethe.[143]

Science is replete with stories of long, passionate struggles that cul-minate in a single moment of insight. The discoverer, seeing through multiplicity and confusion to an elusive coherence and hidden har-mony, experiences an inner illumination. Since we will later be using simple mathematical exercises, as an example of *aperçu*, consider William Rowan Hamilton's discovery of quaternions. We all know the arithmetic of whole numbers (integers), and also of fractions (rational numbers). If we are a bit more sophisticated, we can manipulate non-repeating deci-mals (real numbers) as well. Beyond real numbers, mathematicians have

---

143. Goethe in a letter to Soret of December 30, 1823, quoted by Rike Wankmüller, *Goethes Schriften*, Hamburger Ausgabe, vol. 13, p. 616.

developed *imaginary* and *complex* numbers. Hamilton sought to develop a mathematics of numbers that was one step further still, beyond complex numbers. He offers a beautiful recollection of his discovery of this new type of number, called quaternions, in a letter to his son Archibald.[144]

Each complex numbers can be thought of as composed of two parts or as a pair of numbers. Adding two complex numbers is done by adding the component parts of the pairs to one another. Multiplication is likewise a multiplication of the pairs according to a special rule. Not content to stop there, Hamilton struggled long to determine the addition and multiplication rules for *triplets*. On the sixteenth day of October, 1843, while he was escorting his wife across the Broome Bridge, "an *electric* circuit seemed to *close*; and a spark flashed forth." In that instant, Hamilton could see how to multiply triplets. It would take years for Hamilton and others to elaborate the discovery in detail, but the significance of the perception was immediate. It was expressed in a formula so clear in his mind that he could (and did) carve it out then and there on the wall of the bridge, Hamilton "saw" the solution to the problem, which in this instance was purely mathematical in character. The empirical element in mathematics is not sensory but mental, and it was a realm Hamilton loved. Into his inner world of mental phenomena there suddenly broke

---

144. William Rowan Hamilton, letter of August 5, 1865: "Every morning in the early part of the above-cited month [October 1843], on my coming down to breakfast, your (then) little brother William Edwin, and yourself, used to ask me, 'Well, Papa, can you *multiply* triplets'? Whereto I was always obliged to reply, with a sad shake of the head: 'No, I can only *add* and *subtract* them.' But on the 16th day of the same month—which happened to be a Monday, and a Council day of the Royal Irish Academy—I was walking in to attend and preside, and your mother was walking with me, along the Royal Canal, to which she had perhaps driven; and although she talked with me now and then, yet an *under-current* of thought was going on in my mind, which gave at last a *result*, whereof it is not too much to say that I felt *at once* the importance. An *electric* circuit seemed to *close*; and a spark flashed forth, the herald (as I *foresaw, immediately*) of many long years to come of definitely directed thought and work, by *myself* if spared, and at all events on the part of *others*, if I should even be allowed to live long enough distinctly to communicate the discovery. Nor could I resist the impulse—unphilosophical as it may have been—to cut with a knife on a stone of Brougham Bridge, as we passed it, the fundamental formula with the symbols, i, j, k; namely, $i^2 = j^2 = k^2 = ijk = -1$ which contains the *Solution* of the *Problem*."
http://www.maths.tcd.ie/pub/HistMath/People/Hamilton/Letters/BroomeBridge.html.

the light of insight. His long labors had fashioned a new mathematical organ, and inner illumination "flashed forth."

Mathematical and scientific thoughts can themselves be the subject of reflection, affection, and active investigation. Poetry enters into science by the door of faithful and loving attention, or, as Emerson put it, "All becomes poetry when we look from within... because poetry is science, is the breath of the same spirit by which nature lives. And never did any science originate, but by a poetic perception."[145] Science, ethically pursued, is but one of the many ways that loving can become knowing. Events in life can provide the occasion for moral epiphanies as well as intellectual ones.

In 1893, Mohandas Gandhi, a young Indian lawyer, was traveling on business through South Africa between Durban and Pretoria. Educated at University College, London, and a new member of the British bar, he had purchased a first-class ticket for the long journey. Midway through the journey, another passenger summoned the conductor and insisted that the dark-skinned Gandhi be sent to sit with the "coolies." Gandhi displayed his ticket and refused, whereupon he was forcibly ejected from the train and spend a bitterly cold night in the local train station. During the course of his sleepless night, Gandhi pondered not only his own experience but that of all the colored of South Africa who daily suffered much greater indignities than his own. It was then, he wrote later, that[146]

> I began to think of my duty. Should I fight for my rights or go back to India, or should I go on to Pretoria without minding the insults... The hardship to which I was subjected was only superficial—only a symptom of the deep disease of color prejudice. I should try, if possible, to root out the disease and suffer hardships in the process.

Within one year, Gandhi had founded the Natal Indian Congress to agitate for the rights of Indians, and—inspired by Thoreau's essay on

---

145. Ralph Waldo Emerson, quoted by Peter Antony Obuchowski, Jr., *The Relationship of Emerson's Interest in Science to his Thought*, University of Michigan, Ph.D. 1969 (Ann Arbor, MI: University Microfilms, Inc., 1969), p. 47, and in *The Complete Works of Ralph Waldo Emerson*, ed. Edward Waldo Emerson, vol. 8, pp. 364–65.
146. Mohandas K. Gandhi, *Autobiography: The Story of My Experiments with Truth*, trans. Mahadev Desai (New York: Dover, 1983), p. 97.

the subject—two years later he was teaching nonviolent, passive resistance and civil disobedience. While Gandhi had surely been intellectually aware of racism, his personal experience on the train, coupled with his selfless concern for all those who suffered likewise, led to both insight and action that animated his long life of social activism. Gandhi's study of the law and his concern for justice were never bound to conventional legal codes, which in fact permitted the abuse of "colored people." Instead, he found his way through experience and reflection to a moral insight that transcended the legal conventions of the country in which he was traveling. He also had the faith and determination to lead others to a similar perception. Gandhi had formed the organ suited to a moral insight whose luminous truth trumped those of the law books. He knew that all of humanity possessed the rudiments of that same capacity, but that it needed to be awakened and developed. Gandhi lived his whole life guided by the moral insights directly accessible to him and only secondarily by the statutes of nation states. The light of conscience reaches beyond social convention to a realm of spiritual realities ruled over by love.

To summarize, the nine characteristics of contemplative inquiry are:

1. Respect
2. Gentleness
3. Intimacy
4. Participation
5. Vulnerability
6. Transformation
7. Organ formation
8. Illumination
9. Insight

I view these nine as the essential features of a way of knowing that culminates in a form of cognition I have called contemplative insight. Genuine intellectual, moral, and spiritual insights all share a similar genesis. Whatever their character, we achieve them by means of selfless interest, and ultimately through love.

When he declared that "Love is ever the beginning of Knowledge as fire is of light," Thomas Carlyle emphasized the first four characteristics of contemplative inquiry. These four lead us toward the object of attention, in order that one may gently become one with it, which is to say we practice love. Echoing Goethe, Rudolf Steiner once remarked that "Nothing can reveal itself to us which we do not love." And elsewhere he spoke emphatically of the importance of love as a "force of knowledge."[147] Without this force we cannot go out into the world and participate in it as contemplative inquiry demands that we do. However, in order to attain insight, transformation and illumination are required as well. Our willingness to change makes us vulnerable toward that which is before us. Only in this way can the organs we require be formed. Finally, the proper light of mind, suited to the experience offered us by the organs of cognition, needs to illuminate phenomena with understanding.

An epistemology of love is not divorced from life. Despite many who have argued to the contrary, knowing is not separate from action and ethics. As Parker Palmer has pointed out, "every way of knowing becomes a way of living, every epistemology becomes an ethic."[148] Because of our emphasis on transformation and organ formation, what we know is a reflection of who we are. Only she who has eyes to see and ears to hear will know in the manner described here. Who we are also determines how we act and the ethics we embody. In this way, being, knowing, and acting are invariably interconnected. Like many of us, Palmer is deeply concerned by the dominant epistemology within which we live, which fosters an ethic of violence. By contrast, the ethic associated with an epistemology of love is one we can all live by, and is one that will benefit the world.

Practicing an epistemology of love moves us ever closer to the nature or being of that which we would know. We become intimate with, participate with, and ultimately identify with the object of our attention, knowing it from the inside, and thus are practicing a contemplative form

---

147. Rudolf Steiner: "However, one must cultivate a force of knowledge that in normal life is not taken as a force of knowledge. One must cultivate love as a force of knowledge, to go out selflessly into the things and occurrences of the world." *Anthroposophie Menschenerkenntnis und Medizin* (GA 319), July 17, 1924, p. 153. My translation.

148. Parker Palmer, "The Violence of Our Knowledge: Toward a Spirituality of Higher Education," 21st Century Learning Initiative, http://www.21learn.org/arch/articles/palmer_spirituality.html, a lecture at Berea College (1993).

of inquiry. Through additional exercises we can support this way of knowing and become still clearer about the stages along the way.

From Image to Insight

> *Earth, isn't this what you want:*
>
> *to arise within us,*
>
> *INVISIBLE? Isn't it your dream*
>
> *to be wholly invisible someday?*
>
> — RILKE, NINTH DUINO ELEGY[149]

Behind my house is a cluster of variously colored poppies. They are prolific and beautiful, offering up their delicate, brilliantly colored flowers for a few days before the tissue-like petals fall to the ground. Each blossom is ready to be replaced by new buds that in their turn unfurl on long crooked stems, preparing for the moment when the two halves of the soft, hairy, green coverings fall away to reveal the pigmented petals inside. Every aspect of these poppy plants seems to be at once distinct and yet organically related. Each detail is unique, each phase quite different from the one before. Yet the whole and all its parts participate in the same delicacy and impermanence that is the poppy. In short, it is an organism. I would like to use these poppies as an example of how one can develop contemplative inquiry further, moving from object through inner image to insight in meditation.

As in the nature practices described earlier in this book, one begins by giving one's full attention to the object, here the poppies. Slowly and gently one attends not only to the attractive blossom but also to the other aspects of the plant, large and small: the stem with its soft bristles,

---

149. Translated by Stephen Mitchell, in *The Enlightened Heart*, ed. Stephen Mitchell (New York: Harper & Row, 1989).

the floppy indented leaves, the fragile petals whose colors wave in the wind, the golden center within each blossom.... One looks not so much with the eye of the botanist as with the eye of the artist. Note the subtle differences in color and shape; the specific is of more interest than the general at this phase. Take time and repeat the observations over some days so that the poppies become a part of your inner life, until you can easily and accurately recall their image. As with a poem committed to memory, you can enjoy them through recollection nearly as much as by sitting near them in the garden.

Having attended to them in this way, we turn inward. We create a vivid sustained mental image of the poppies, or even of a single poppy, and work with it, detail by detail, to enhance its quality of presence in our mind. After it has been fully present in us for a time, we inwardly set the mental image of the poppy aside and practice open attention in perfect stillness, without image or object, without grasping or longing, without expectation or thought. If an afterimage or echo emerges as a soul gesture in the stillness, we should not mentally reach for it or try to understand the meaning of the appearance. Instead we maintain open attention and practice wonder, gratitude, and admiration for whatever appears as inner image. It may be a mere inner gesture, a subtle form, a bodily sensation, or a color experience. Through repeated cognitive breathing exercises, an inner world is cultivated that corresponds to the meditative objects with an increasingly rich and exact imagination. Arbitrary fantasy is of no interest to us. Rather, through exercises such as this one, we are patiently developing a soul faculty that can respond to outer sensory stimuli in an objective interior way. Syllable by syllable the outer language of the sense world is translated into the inner language of soul. With time this world of interior experience can become a vivid and beautiful part of one's life. This is what makes the next step so difficult.

In order to move from image to insight, one must find the strength to set aside the glories of imagination for what appears at first to be a barren void. In the language of the triangle exercise, we will attempt to move from the constantly changing image of the triangle to the living concept of the triangle experienced as pure activity that is embodied in the particular triangles. The living concept "triangle" is a single type of activity capable of manifold expressions (i.e., all triangles). In the case of the blossoming poppy we suppress the image and attend to the thought active in us (and in the poppy), which is "blossoming poppy." Here we confront a truly difficult stage in the practice. When the memory image and even the afterimage fall away, what is left? In order to cognize the blossoming poppy we must have been thinking it. Our activity of mind had a distinctive character, and it is this we want. Turn to the activity, leaving all images aside. In this way we practice seeing through outer and inner phenomena to the activity behind their appearance. The practice of cultivating insight consists of suppressing the world of images and seeking the spiritual activities behind or within the images.

One aid to experiencing the activity behind the image is to build up consciously the mental image of a blossoming poppy. Forming a specific image requires us to tap the generative source for that particular image. Normally we do this unconsciously, but in meditation we can become aware of the hitherto unnoticed origins of our images and ideas. Having created the image of a blossoming poppy, we shift our attention from the image to the source used to imagine it. In doing this we discover the thought-activity "blossoming poppy." In forming the poppy image we enact or embody its associated thought activity. The type of enaction was particular to the poppy; otherwise something different would have appeared to our mind. When distracted we fail to direct our own thought activity and images appear in uncontrolled profusion. In the above meditation, not only do we fully control our thoughts, but we also observe the specific kind of activity needed for imagining a blossoming poppy. As with the triangle, the living concept of "blossoming poppy" does not look like a poppy, but we do recognize it as the blossoming-poppy-thought. If you find this exercise difficult, you are not alone. We are accustomed to thinking reactively. Poppies show up in our field of view; we recognize their delightful presence and name them. Perhaps we study them for a moment or two. If we remember them, again we delight in the memory, recognize them, and go on. By meditating the poppies, however, we are doing something different.

We first move from object to image, by which I do not mean the memory image or a fantasy, but the inner, soul afterimage of the object. In this schema I term this soul impression the "inner image." The *inner image* is what arises in Weil's "void" through cognitive breathing. We may use the object itself or a mental image of the object to evoke the afterimage. In the second stage we take the inner image as the focus of our attention in cognitive breathing. After living with the inner image, we turn our mental gaze away from it and open our attention a second time to allow a second void to appear. In doing so, we shift our awareness from the inner image to the thought activity that is the source of the inner image. To stress its immaterial nature, I will term it "spiritual activity." At this stage, both the outer object and the inner image have been left behind, and we sense the pure generative activity that gives rise to them.

In the final stage the meditant practices cognitive breathing a third time. Spiritual activity suggests a source or agent. One takes that activity as the object of focused attention and then allows the activity to disappear as well. In the void of open awareness, agency or being arises. No sense of separation from the agent remains. The meditant is, perhaps only briefly at first, one with the agent in an I-Thou unification. In the Asian traditions this is termed "non-dual" awareness, in which subject and object distinctions all vanish.

The meditative sequence is:[150]

1.   Object
2.   Inner Image
3.   Spiritual Activity
4.   Agency/Being

Suppose you chanced on a painter in her studio, fully engaged in the creative process. The canvas is before her, brushes are in hand. She is glancing back and forth between the *object* she is painting and the *image* on the canvas, dabbing at her palette and applying paint to the painting. Her *activity* is bringing about the painting as image. The *being* of the painting as it lives in her has given rise to her activity, and so to the image as well. The object that she is painting is the fruit of a similar process. In a spiritual imagination of the universe, there is a mind in nature as well as in the human being. We are not the sole agents in the world. We create

---

150. Rudolf Steiner, *Stages of Higher Knowledge*, trans. Lisa D. Monges and Floyd McKnight (Spring Valley, NY: Anthroposophic Press, 1967).

paintings, but a world mind makes the world. World mind is the agent whose activity results in sense objects. We need not posit a remote realm of Platonic forms, but only allow for more and more subtle realms of spiritual phenomena and insight.

In the figure below I have put the sequence into diagrammatic form. In doing so I show that the transition between stages is made via the lemniscates of cognitive breathing. What was afterimage at one stage becomes the object of meditative attention at the next. The afterimage of inner image, for example, is spiritual activity. Activity in turn becomes the object of focused attention, which yields agency or being as afterimage.[151]

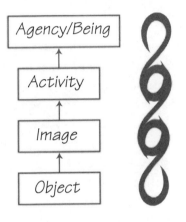

Why bother going through all four stages? The meditative path I have described is arduous, but the rewards are significant at each stage of the journey. It is, in essence, a research method intended to lead one to genuine insights not confined to the physical senses. Rilke urged us to be patient, and to love and "live the questions." Through contemplative inquiry we live ever more deeply into the questions, and so change ourselves that we can live the answers also. "And," wrote Rilke, "the point is to live everything."[152]

---

151. Steiner terms the three forms of cognition associated with levels two, three, and four: Imagination, Inspiration, and Intuition.
152. Rilke, *Letters to a Young Poet.*

If we aspire to understand our own essential nature, then we require a method such as the one outlined here. To achieve contemplative knowing, we need to find a basis for cognition that is suited to the beings we are, and to the being of nature. Toward this end, the first exercises in this book are designed to enhance attentional and emotional stability, while the later exercises are intended to destabilize us. They are designed to shake our fixed hold on a reality that is grounded in sense experience alone. The move from outer image to afterimage is a first step away from the sense world and towards an inner response.

We cannot rest here, however. If we do, we give ourselves over to a delightful, expansive domain of ever-changing inner impressions that can distract us from life—a sort of inner equivalent to TV and video games, which distract us enough already in their external forms! Therefore, I want to strongly emphasize that I am not seeking to supplant sense reality with a fanciful if glorious world of inner experiences. Rather, our journey to the spiritual aspects of self and world takes place through contemplative work with material drawn from nature and great world teachings. This work moves us from the outer dimensions of the meditated material and shifts our awareness stepwise to its essential spiritual core. In this way we are safeguarded from the very real dangers of projection and delusion. The end we seek is insight that can serve us in life, making us more fit to address the problems we meet with deep multifaceted understanding that does not spring from instrumental reason alone. The fruit of contemplative inquiry should be a wisdom born in freedom that can serve love.

The Practice of Contemplative Inquiry

Even given the preceding sketch of the stages leading from image to insight, the concrete practice of contemplative inquiry remains quite open. It can be done in various ways, and I urge you to explore methods you find useful. One way of starting is to select a theme or question with which you would like to work. Examples range from the personal to the global, from the scientific to the artistic. They might include: Why do I always argue with my best friend? Or, What is the nature of fundamentalism? Or, How can I work with this particular autistic child? In many instances, however, it is not a question but a theme or area of interest that engages us.

For example, one might wish to study meditatively the processes at work in the unfolding leaf, or the growing child, or the work of Rembrandt, or a sonata by Beethoven. One longs to become more intimate with and insightful about such things. Contemplative inquiry can be a great aid.

Having chosen the theme or question, one takes up the particular phenomenon. If one is concerned for an autistic child, one begins by carefully considering the child's behavior, outer features, and speech. The full range of outer signs is lovingly gathered. Often it helps to journal about these such that they become the center of our interest. We bring to them the calm, clear attention we have developed in the inner hygiene exercises so that we may give the autistic child our full attention without emotional distraction. I term this the stage of *outer phenomenology*. During this part of the practice, we fully attend to the outer phenomena of the question or theme we have selected for contemplative inquiry. One can easily imagine how a work of art or object from nature might be studied in a similar way. Everything has its outer phenomenological aspect, even in pure philosophy or mathematics.

After completing an outer phenomenological study, one shifts to an *inner phenomenology*. We are concerned not only with the outer behavior of the autistic child but also with a comprehensive study of his or her inner experiences. Through our cultivated faculties of empathy, we do not merely observe from the outside but enter into the child's life and participate in it. Our own feelings begin to mirror the feelings of the child across from us. Cognitive-affective neuroscience has recently documented the profound social and emotional intelligence we humans possess.[153] Compelling research indicates that we are deeply social beings with amazing powers of empathy and social understanding. When the findings of neuroscience are expanded by an enlarged spiritual view of the human being, our appreciation of these capacities is only increased. We can return to our journal to record the inner phenomena we are able to sense at play. This is, of course, a delicate area, one into which our own sympathies and antipathies can readily intrude. However, if we have balanced our inner life carefully, using, for example, the six exercises

---

153. Daniel Goleman, *Social Intelligence* (New York: Bantam, 2006).

of chapter three, then we are highly unlikely to allow our own emotions unconsciously to become confused with the feelings of the other. In the case of a work of art, our well-schooled feeling response is essential; this is the arena in which we practice an inner phenomenology.

Having completed both outer and inner phenomenological studies, we can form a content for focused, meditative attention out of our observations. In chapters four and five the content for meditation was taken from nature, from sacred verses and images, or from spiritual narratives. Contemplative inquiry asks us to form an appropriate content for meditation out of our own observations concerning the theme or question under study. We compose the meditation we will then use in a cognitive breathing exercise. From our careful outer and inner observations we write a line or phrase suitable for placing into the left side of the lemniscate of focused attention. Together with words we may also wish to sketch a few lines that indicate in form what we have observed outwardly and inwardly. Each of us, whether or not we are a practiced artist, can create a simple form that reflects our intimate observations.

By way of a simple example, I once took as the subject of my contemplative inquiry a problematic aspect of a particular relationship. I practiced outer and inner phenomenology and then composed these few words and associated sketch.

From difference

to dogma and despair;

why us? Why apart?

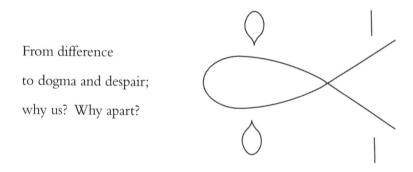

The words we write and sketch we draw become the focus of our attention. They are taken up into a cognitive breathing process of the sort we are now very familiar with. In the language I have introduced previously, the words and sketch are taken as the object from which an inner image will arise. The inner image is the afterimage generated by the words and sketch we have composed. As we move back and forth between focused and open attention, the inner image gradually strengthens to the point where it can become the basis for the next stage of the contemplative inquiry process. The inner image itself now becomes the object of our focused attention, and we seek the spiritual activity behind and within it through open awareness. Finally, if we come so far, we can again shift awareness through a third cognitive breathing process in which we seek to rise to the "being" of the question or issue. (See the previous diagram.) At this point the agency producing the particular situation we started with is encountered and known from the inside. In Goethe's language we have risen to the level of "true theory," or the *aperçu*, which we also recognize as the level of genuine insight.

Plant as Proteus

The botanical studies of Jochen Bockemühl can be understood from the perspective of contemplative inquiry. His phenomenological, Goethean method of studying plant metamorphosis moves explicitly from image to insight, identifying the spiritual activities at work in plant development.

My previous treatment of form and movement used the pristine forms of geometry, but the transformations we encountered in that context can be found again in plant metamorphosis. The Greek god Proteus could take on any shape, and Goethe saw the plant—especially the leaf—as protean because of the infinite variations it could manifest. Yet every variant was guided by the single idea of the plant species to which it belonged. Goethe termed this guiding agent the "archetypal plant" and insisted to Schiller that it was no mere abstract idea but something he could experience directly. Through his extensive study of plants, Goethe had worked his way through the stages outlined above to the level of agency/being.

Two powerful concepts animated Goethe's work, particularly in the sciences: polarity and intensification (*Steigerung*). We can use these as an entryway for a sequence of contemplative exercises that will move us from abstract geometric forms to meditative insight concerning plant metamorphosis. In an elaboration of Goethe's botanical studies, Jochen Bockemühl has researched plant leaf metamorphosis using Goethe's method. It provides an elegant introduction to the dynamic principles of polarity and intensification in botany.[154] Botanical study is best done directly from the plant in nature, but, since that possibility is not available to us, we will work from drawings. Our study of these will be superficial in comparison to the full treatment accorded them by Bockemühl but will suffice for our particular purpose.

At the simplest level, we first observe how the tiny seed leaves push through the soil into the sunlight and air. Over time the plant grows and its leaves increase in size; the plant expands in space as it gains in height. Its lateral appendages reach their fullest extension and then begin to contract; the plant's leaves diminish in size as the flower bud forms at the end of the plant stalk. The figure below shows the leaves of a corn salad plant (*valerianella locusta*) from seed leaves to those below the blossom.

In a sudden expansive burst, the flower opens, later to contract again to fruit and seed. Following this sequence with our mind's eye, we see that the plant begins in its most contracted form, the seed. It expands over time into a full growth of foliage, then contracts to bud and expands again into flower. Finally the plant comes full circle, contracting to fruit and seed. Expansion and contraction thus form the polarity between which the plant grows. We can think of these as polar activities that animate the plant in different measure during different phases of its life cycle.

---

154. Jochen Bockemühl, "Transformation in the Foliage Leaves of the Higher Plants." *Goethe's Way of Science*, ed. David Seamon and Arthur Zajonc (Albany, NY: SUNY Press, 1998), Chapter 6; Frederick Amrine, "Goethean Method in the Work of Jochen Bockemühl," *Goethe and the Sciences: A Reappraisal*, ed. Frederick Amrine, Francis J. Zucker, and Harvey Wheeler (Dordrecht, Holland: D. Reidel, 1987), pp. 301–18.

In addition to this simple polarity, the plant appears to strive upward, adding an axis of "intensification" to the process of growth, flowering, and fruiting. As the leaves develop they spiral around the axis of upright growth, expanding and then pulling back as the moment of inflorescence approaches. The flower marks a crescendo and climax, with the fruit and seed a coda to the harmonious interweaving of the varied voices: expansion, contraction, and intensification. The musical metaphor is, I think, particularly apt. Simultaneously through all of nature there play multiple formative activities, which we can come to experience as several voices in a polyphonic harmony. Through even such simple plant observations, we can learn to experience in the botanical phenomena themselves the activities of expansion, contraction, and intensification.

To this Bockemühl adds a great deal of refinement. Focusing on the metamorphosis of foliage leaves in higher plants, he identifies four specific activities that interplay in varied ways throughout the lifetime of the plant, like the four voices in a chorale. Bockemühl attends to the qualities of form and to the generative movements that seem to live between the individual leaf forms. In this way we shift our attention from the formal elements of the leaf, such as petiole and blade, and focus instead on the transformations of the leaf forms. The emphasis is on movement instead of stasis, on activity instead of the stable elements. The question changes to, what are the kinds of movements or qualities of transformation present in the foliage leaves? Bockemühl identifies four fundamental activities: "shooting," "articulating," "spreading," and "stemming." As the leaves develop sequentially, these four processes are active in various degrees. Their timing and relative strength determine the particular form of the leaf at any given time. No attempt is made to track these transformative processes back to gene expression or other mechanisms; rather, Bockemühl remains phenomenological throughout.

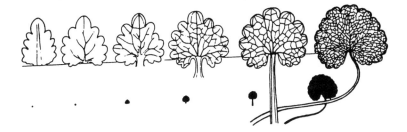

Consider the case of ground-ivy above. In the top sequence the individual leaves have been magnified to show the increase in complexity; in the lower sequence the scale is unchanging in order to show the increase in physical size. Shooting is the first dominant activity, but the processes of articulating and spreading also add their characteristics early on. In the early stages look also at the base of the leaf and note that the leaf form extends downward; this marks the continuation of shooting and articulating until the fourth stage. At this point the process of spreading intensifies, and the leaf fills out with no further shooting or articulating. The leaf veins multiply and the rounded form of the leaf is complete, with stemming and spreading continuing until the final phase.

In Bockemühl's version of Goethean observation, one seeks for the life processes or formative activities that animate and form the growth of higher plant foliage. The formative activities are quite specific, and each operates during particular periods of the plant's development, often in concert with another. The meditative practices in which we have been interested school us in moving from the image to the activity in a manner that is analogous to moving from the image of the leaf to the activities that form it.[155]

If you have built your own home, then you know the feeling of being deeply engaged in a creative process. If you are an artist, then the thrill of creativity is familiar to you. Once the house is complete or the artwork is finished, a certain life departs from the site or studio. We have all felt the vitality that comes with the creative process, and it can be one of our greatest joys in life. All around us are finished works, but Bockemühl wants to help us move from these finished works to the creative activity and formative life processes that generate them. The transition from viewing finished forms to discovering the activities that produce them is a key accomplishment in the spiritual journey. A comprehensive understanding of the world around us requires this advance. The contemplative comes to comprehend not an object but an activity. Objects have contours and color; activities also have definite characteristics that

---

155. In Rudolf Steiner's language this is the transition from what he terms Imagination to Inspiration.

distinguish one from another. Bockemühl succeeded in articulating the different activities required for development in higher plants, but activities of diverse kinds are behind everything. Each possesses its own distinguishing gesture, which we must learn to cognize.

Thinking Life

The British writer and philosopher Owen Barfield has drawn our attention to the old scholastic distinction made first by John Scottus Eriugena in the ninth century and which was important to Coleridge, namely the difference between *natura naturata* ("nature natured") and *natura naturans* ("nature naturing").[156] The distinction is precisely that drawn above between passive nature and active nature, between the inert objects that surround us and the activities or processes that bring them into being. Bockemühl's exercises, as well as the geometric exercises presented earlier, are designed to move us from object to activity. By enacting this change, we shift our awareness to a process-level of reality—a domain of activity and relationship—in which everything is in relationship and movement, everything is shifting from potential to actual and back again. And agency/being stands behind it all.

Goethe appreciated the importance of this level of reality when he wrote, "The highest that we receive from God and nature is Life."[157] Because it is extremely difficult to truly think "life," we often settle for its fossilized remains. "The concept of arising is completely denied us. Therefore, when we see something becoming, we think that it already has become," writes Goethe elsewhere.[158] In order to comprehend nature in the act of "naturing," we require a high mode of knowing termed by Goethe *Vernunft* (reason), which he contrasted with a more practical or instrumental form of understanding called *Verstand*. He wrote of these, "Reason [*Vernunft*] is suited to what is developing or becoming

---

156. Owen Barfield, *What Coleridge Thought* (Middletown, CT: Wesleyan University Press, 1971), Chapter 2.
157. Goethe, *Hamburger Ausgabe*, vol. 12, (Munich: C. H. Beck, 1982), p. 396 (Maxim 227).
158. Goethe, *Hamburger Ausgabe*, vol. 8, p. 477 (Maxim 108).

[*Werdende*], instrumental understanding [*Verstand*] to what is already developed [*Gewordene*]. Reason rejoices in development, instrumental understanding wishes to hold all things fast in order to use them."[159] In order to succeed at contemplative inquiry we need to develop in us the capacity of true reason that, as Rudolf Steiner puts it, "leads back to reality" and is the capacity by which we perceive active ideas.[160] The *aperçu* or moment of direct perception is an occasion when reason, in the sense meant here, is active. It is synthetic and illuminating, a high kind of seeing, as Emerson wrote of it. Through it we are caught up in the circuit of things, that is, in their harmonious relationships and ceaseless movement, metamorphosis, and creativity: *natura naturans*.

Traditional cultures such as the Native American Indians possessed a natural capacity for participation in this process-level of reality. Barfield called it "original participation."[161] We find evidence of original participation, for example, in the languages of Native peoples. Like many Native languages, Navajo is a process or verb-oriented language, in contrast to modern Western languages, which are predominantly object or noun-oriented. In Navajo, many noun-meanings are given by verbs, which can become quite complex. A typical example is the Navajo word *łééʼiiʼniłł*, "cemetery," which is actually a verb meaning "they lie in the ground." In addition, Navajo grammar reflects the degree of "animacy" of the object, with humans possessing the most animacy, while natural forces and abstractions embody the least.[162] The entire emphasis in Navajo and similar Native languages appears to be on life, action, and process. I view this as a remnant or reflection of their original participation in the process-level of reality. Today, in order to regain access to the process-level, we must consciously undertake specific contemplative exercises. These lead to what Barfield calls "final participation," in which the human being recaptures the ancient participatory mode of awareness,

159. Goethe, *Hamburger Ausgabe*, vol. 12, p. 438 (Maxim 538).

160. Rudolf Steiner, *Goethe's Theory of Knowledge: An Outline of the Epistemology of His Worldview*, Chapter 12.

161. Owen Barfield, *Saving the Appearances* (Middletown, CT: Wesleyan University Press, 1988).

162. http://www.answers.com/topic/navajo-language.

but now with the hard-won self-consciousness and technical mastery of the world common to a modern person. Accomplishing this, we attain a form of sustained wakefulness that can dwell inside the life from which all is born and into which all returns, and we can acknowledge the truth of Rumi's lines: "Anyone who loves Your making is full of Glory. Anyone who loves what You have made is not a true believer."[163]

Becoming the Other

Imagine a person not known to you before, standing quietly in front of you. At first, the person is only an image, an enigma. Suddenly the person begins to act and speak. Through those actions and speech you discover something about the person's intentions, thoughts, and concerns. You start to know the person for the first time. The greater the range of action and speech, the more clearly is the person's nature revealed. Every playwright and novelist knows that action and dialogue bring characters to life.

In like fashion, by shifting in meditation from image to activity, we take a huge step forward in knowledge. The image may be beautiful or ugly, simple or complex, but its significance is lost on us until we reach beyond image to the activity behind it. But one stage further remains on the path of knowledge we have set out upon: direct intuition of the being or agent whose activity we already know. Although the world's spiritual traditions speak of it often, nothing is more difficult to achieve, or even to describe, than the direct, non-dual apprehension of the other. As soon as one uses language, one is already using a dualistic mode of expression. Representation of any type is the negation of pure participation, which is the proper modality for non-dual awareness. Yet, if we are to offer a complete description of the path of contemplative inquiry, we must attempt to gain some idea of the final, fourth stage that I have termed agency/being.

Emerson wrote that the poet's form of knowing "does not come by study, but by the intellect being where and what it sees." I am normally

---

163. Jelaluddin Rumi, *Mathnawi*, III, 1360–61, *This Longing*, trans. Coleman Barks and John Moyne (Putney, VT: Threshold Books, 1988), p. 52.

not either where or what you are. I am outside you, and I have a different nature. Perhaps you are a woman and I am a man, you are young and I am old, you are an artist and I am a scientist. Emerson maintains, however, that a poet so "resigns" himself to the nature of things that he gives up his identity completely and becomes the other. This can occur because he is a lover, and lovers are capable of the apparently impossible, namely of losing the self for the sake of the other. In Merton's language, one sets aside the social self and becomes the silent self. All conventional ego identity must vanish if the universal not-I is to emerge. Loss of self and love are the linked prerequisites for becoming where and what the other is.

Becoming the other is the greatest mystery. Outside and inside, subject and object disappear. Who am I? You! What am I? All things! In Asia one speaks of the Buddha-nature that is in all things; in the West we might term it Logos, Word, the Christ. Becoming the other requires that we find the Logos-nature in us and so in the world. Only then can we know from the inside, through identifying completely and utterly with the other. We no longer view the other from the outside, but know the other as we now know ourselves. Of course, the other can be anything. Our knowing of a tree, a river, a person, can all be non-dual. The Logos-nature is the nature of all things, not human beings only.

We have hints of such knowing in normal life. Loving concern can shift our awareness for a moment such that we forget ourselves and live into another person's situation. We may feel what the other feels, anticipate his or her thoughts and actions. In such moments our own actions are not guided by self-interest but by our compassionate interest in the other. On such occasions, loving has become a way of knowing that leads to moral action.

To achieve non-dual knowing requires that we let go even of activity, which still separates us from that which is to be known. The actions of a person reveal a great deal, but they are not the person. The activities in the poppy plant are not the archetypal plant. Having lived fully and attentively in the actions of the other, having come to love the other, one lets go of activity to dwell again in the space of open attention, the void. But now *all* sense of self vanishes. We lose every last trace of the grounding offered to us by the conventional ego. We are, in the fullest sense of the word: nothing. We die. But, as Goethe says, unless you are ready to die, you cannot become. Die and become: this is the hallmark of direct intuitive understanding. Through Logos, one becomes the tree, river, or person. One becomes the beloved. And through the preparation of contemplative activity, one can take this step without succumbing to fear.

I began this book with the theme of deepening solitude, so much a part of the contemplative life. With this concluding accomplishment, one of greatest solitude, the human being is simultaneously connected to all of creation. The separations that characterize human life fall completely away and gentle, selfless love prevails.

Within Wisdom

Consider one final exercise that we can take through the four stages given above—from object through image to activity, and finally to agency. We take as the object of our attention not something drawn from nature, but a line often given by Rudolf Steiner as well suited for meditation.[164] Contemplate the sentence, "Wisdom lives in the light." Sound the words, aloud or inwardly, allowing them to permeate your awareness, appreciating their mystery. The elements of wisdom and life are not manifest to the physical senses like the poppy, but their meaning is familiar to us nonetheless. Regularly sounding the words of the meditation to ourselves, settling our attention on them and their meanings, in itself can positively affect our inner life. Having worked actively with the line for a time, giving it our undivided attention, we can change our meditative posture and open our awareness to silence and stillness. In doing so, we create the space for grace and for the soul echo of the words within us. Silently, we welcome what arises. In this manner we move from the words themselves to what I have been calling the afterimage or inner image. If we wish to go beyond the afterimage experience to spiritual activity, we must take a further step. We suppress the feelings and experiences that arise in the open space as afterimage, and we turn to the activity that is its source.

How can we do this? In meditation, create an open space empty of all objects or activities. If wisdom were to presence itself in that space,

---

164. Rudolf Steiner, *Self-Transformation* (London: Rudolf Steiner Press, 1995), p. 148.

what would need to change? What activity would need to be present there? Resist the temptation to look for some *thing*; rather, sense the kind of activity that would connote wisdom. Attend to it, gently, as content and reality. You have recognized the presence of wisdom as pure activity. Now allow your space of attention to be also a place where light is present. By this I don't mean that you should experience the space as bright. Remember that the depths of outer space, although full of light, appear dark to the eye. So too here, the space of your imagination is full of light, but need not be outwardly bright. Sense the activity of light in your space of attention. The words of the meditation are "Wisdom lives in the light." These words ask us to place wisdom livingly in the light, one activity into another. Wisdom is in the light not as water in a glass, but like a human is in his or her body.

In this meditation we learn that each of its words—wisdom, lives, in, light—has a characteristic activity we can discern inwardly. As we become familiar with their characteristic activities, then even in the absence of the sound or script that represents them, we will be able to recognize their presence. Now the significance of contemplative insight should be clear. As meditation deepens we awaken to experiences that have no outer representation. Images may arise, but interpretation using the reactive instrumental thinking of normal consciousness (*natura naturata*) would lead to error. Awakened consciousness will use fragments of memory and conventional consciousness, but its meanings can be read only by foregoing the logic of gravity, by suppressing the image and seeking insight through participation in activity.

It takes time to become familiar with this new realm and to develop an active or living way of thinking that is capable of new knowledge. We come to insight here not through recognition of sense images, but rather by cognizing dynamic spiritual activities. Then, in the fourth stage, the activities of wisdom and life that we know through participation lead back to agencies. The final stage of the path takes us from activity to being. The form of intuitive cognition required here is unlike ratiocination or logical argumentation. It is a direct apprehension, a moment of discovery, an indwelling, an epiphany. Instead of "looking through a glass darkly," we know directly, face to face. Goethe termed this moment the *aperçu*; the Greeks called it *epistēmē*; the Buddhists called it "direct perception." Every tradition honors this high moment that is simultaneously an achievement long worked for, and an instance of unexpected grace and love. Every deep and true insight shares this lineage.

The path of contemplative inquiry is a path of knowledge, but the knowledge we seek is inclusive of the immaterial realities of soul and spirit. In no way does contemplative knowing diminish or contravene conventional science, even if it rejects certain metaphysical assumptions commonly held by many scientists. Nor are the methods of contemplative inquiry unsupported by philosophy, as long as that philosophy remains open to the full dimension of human experience and insight. It remains for us to bring the fruits of contemplative inquiry home.

Bringing It Home

Contemplative practice not only changes who we are but also how we act in the world. The meditative work we have done in solitude begins to affect our lives in increasingly important ways. The very way we are present in the world and with others shifts; the tone of our interactions becomes more patient, generous, and creative. Our practice of meditatively living into experiences, words, and images carries over into life, and we listen more deeply to the views of others, not threatened by diversity and difference. Open to others, we are simultaneously more secure in ourselves, and nature's offerings are more fully appreciated.

Having strengthened and balanced our inner lives, we are better able to carry the illnesses and conflicts that affect all our lives. We are more resilient human beings, more capable because we can bring more of who we really are into life. Our habitual patterns of thought and behavior have been broken, our fears overcome, and so we are more original and creative.

Contemplative practice has affected my life in many ways—some obvious and others subtle. My teaching has become increasingly informed by contemplation. In teaching college physics, I look for experiments and experiences over which I can linger with my students so they and I can live more fully into them. We will pause, take time for reflection, ponder their significance. I relish the philosophical implications of quantum mechanics, and I use quantum paradoxes as koans to challenge the thinking of my students.[165] I value the opportunity to train their attention and flexibility in thinking using the remarkable problems we meet.

In my interdisciplinary classes on science and the humanities, we make time for explicit contemplative practice both in class and outside it. Not only does this benefit students generally by developing their attention and emotional balance, but by linking the practices to the themes of the class, we bring a new modality of inquiry—contemplative inquiry—to what we are studying. Students appreciate it as a different and valuable approach.

Through my work with the Center for Contemplative Mind in Society, I have been able to work with many hundreds of academics throughout North America.[166] We share the ways in which we have found contemplative pedagogy to be of value in our teaching, and have gradually become a community with common concerns. When we come together we do more than present to one another; we also practice together. Since academics don't often sit in silence together, our practice time together is special indeed.

I have found another forum for this work with graduate students and post-doctoral fellows in the sciences and philosophy of science. Between 1998 and 2003, four colleagues and I held two-week summer schools for graduate students in the sciences and the philosophy of science. During that period we worked with nearly one hundred graduate students on scientific and philosophical topics that we felt were inadequately addressed in the standard curriculum. More specifically, we studied the relationship between science and values, and explored aesthetic, moral, and contemplative ways of knowing, in addition to the methods of science. To facilitate this work, the five of us founded the Kira Institute.[167] We were and remain a diverse group including Piet Hut, astrophysicist from Princeton's Institute for Advanced Study, Roger Shepard, cognitive psychologist from Stanford, Bas van Fraassen, philosopher from Princeton University, Steven Tainer, teacher of Asian contemplative traditions, and

---

165. See for example my book with George Greenstein, *Quantum Challenge*, 2nd ed. (Sudbury, MA: Jones & Bartlett, 2006), and *The New Physics and Cosmology: Dialogues with the Dalai Lama* (New York: Oxford University Press, 2004).
166. For details see www.contemplativemind.org.
167. For details see www.kira.org.

myself. In addition to our academic credentials, each of us had, in our own way, sought to complement our academic training with reflective, contemplative, or spiritual practices.

From major universities around the world, graduate students came to the Kira summer schools because they were in some measure dissatisfied with the standard treatment of science and philosophy. Kira's students came with the questions, "Is there a viable alternative to the purely reductive philosophies and materialistic metaphysics of the Anglo-American tradition?" And: "Is there a way that philosophy can once again perform its high task of seeking wisdom?"[168] During our two weeks together, the Kira faculty attempted to sketch the shape of that alternative.

For centuries, Buddhist and Indian philosophers labored tirelessly to articulate an epistemology that met the needs of monk/scholars seeking enlightenment.[169] Like them, we should seek a theory of knowing that is not only capacious enough to include scientific knowing of material existence, but is also adequate to the immaterial experiences associated with contemplative inquiry. Only such a philosophy can act as foundation and guide for us as we seek to extend our knowledge to include the soul-spiritual dimensions of our world. Several twentieth-century figures have worked in this direction, including Whitehead, Bergson, Steiner, and Aurobindo. We need to add our contributions to theirs.

In addition to working toward reform within mainstream institutions of higher education, I have also teamed up with certain academic colleagues to create a new institution of higher education. In 2006 an accredited master's degree program was founded by Robert McDermott and myself as the Owen Barfield School of Sunbridge College.[170] The Barfield School is committed to the integration of academic study, contemplative inquiry, and social ideals. Students with a wide range of

---

168. Pierre Hadot brilliantly reconstructs ancient Greek philosophy as spiritual practice in *What Is Ancient Philosophy*, trans. Michael Chase (Cambridge, MA: Harvard University Press, 2002), and *Philosophy as a Way of Life*, trans. Michael Chase, ed. Arnold I. Davidson (Malden, MA: Blackwell Pub., 1995).
169. See for example Georges Dreyfus, *Recognizing Reality* (Albany, NY: SUNY Press, 1997).
170. For details see www.barfieldschool.org.

interests come together in order to learn interdisciplinary and contemplative ways of investigating the issues they care about most, ranging from education to mathematics, from contemplative movement to art history. All Barfield School faculty combine a professional competency in their field with a long-standing commitment to spiritual and contemplative study. Barfield is indeed a graduate school for contemplative minds.

In my own research, I have selected topics in the foundations of quantum mechanics that offer me the occasion to explore the limits of conventional scientific analysis. I bring to my work the methods of investigation I have attempted to outline in this book. Again and again I find that the problems I am struggling to understand in physics and the philosophy of science are illuminated through contemplative practice.

These are some of the ways in which I have brought contemplative practice home. If my personal experience can be taken as representative, I believe that practice can be of profound personal and social benefit. When properly undertaken, contemplation supports our inner life in multiple ways, and through contemplative inquiry, it opens new doorways of exploration through which we can gain insights and intentions that truly help.

Perhaps I can tell one final story of my own in this regard. In 1994 I had the first of what would be several meetings with the Dalai Lama to discuss philosophical issues arising from the new physics. The Columbia University gathering included an audience of about sixty people, and my then-fourteen-year-old son Tristan was one of the guests. Each mealtime we would get together and talk about the day's events. Tristan's comments were always perceptive, his judgments spot-on, his suggestions for better questions intriguing. He also shared with me an experience he had had sitting at the back of the room that had especially struck him. At one point in the dialogue session, the Dalai Lama was scanning the crowd, the sea of heads parted, and he and Tristan caught one another's eyes. The Dalai Lama leaned forward slightly and waved. Tristan said that in that exchange he felt a "presence" like none he had felt before.

Hearing his story, and carrying it with me through the weekend, I saw how valuable it would be for teenagers to have an opportunity of the kind I was having. Why, I thought, shouldn't they have their own meetings with the Dalai Lama? I immediately sat down and typed up an imagination of how such meetings might be organized. They should not be too large—perhaps up to two hundred young people at a time, I thought. The attendees might be delegates from their schools or communities where the Dalai Lama's ideas would be studied. I began to show my proposal to friends, and before long I came in contact with Dawn Engle and Ivan Suvanjieff. They were considering a similar idea, so the three of us teamed up for the first years of what would become PeaceJam, a youth organization that brings twelve Nobel Peace Laureates together with teens. In the last ten years over 500,000 young people have participated in some way in PeaceJam.[171]

My son lit up when he encountered the "presence" of a contemplative. I recognized that feeling, and thought that face-to-face meetings, rather than books or celebrity events, might also light up the hearts and minds of young people everywhere. I recognized that alone I could do nothing. Yet perhaps I could join my thoughts and efforts with others' to develop an idea. Remarkably, the universe collaborated, and PeaceJam was the fruit. Paying attention, setting a selfless resolve, finding others, and working through the obstacles to success are all part of bringing contemplative practice to life in the world. In our days, the road to holiness does indeed pass through the world of action. I am grateful to all those with whom I have worked and from whom I have learned on my journey into contemplative life.

---

171. See www.peacejam.org.

"An outstanding contribution to addressing a root issue of our time: how to integrate the quest for scientific clarity, contemplative awakening, and improved personal practices in a way that is clear, integrates Eastern and Western wisdom traditions, and offers readers practical methods and tools. It is highly recommended for everyone who wants to deepen their personal foundations for profound change and presencing-based leadership work."

OTTO SCHARMER, MIT
author of *Theory U: Leading from the Future as It Emerges*

"A profound and masterful exposition of the calling, challenges, and above all, the immediate and the harder-to-extract-but-worth-it gifts of meditative inquiry. Disciplining our unruly minds with marvelous exercises in attention and apperception that use all the senses and intelligences available to us, Arthur Zajonc employs his great skill as a teacher, his loving prose, and his razor-sharp intellect to guide us in the experience of a compassionate practice of knowing. Following his path, we can develop and bring to the fore the full dimensionality of our humanness, for ourselves and for others. A glistening gem of a book."

JON KABAT-ZINN
author of *Coming to Our Senses and Arriving at Your Own Door*

"In this beautifully written work, Arthur Zajonc, a seasoned meditator in the Anthroposophical tradition, offers gentle and wise guidance on the path of contemplative inquiry. Drawing both on the writings of Rudolf Steiner and on the world's spiritual traditions, he presents universal truths that are relevant to all contemplative paths, East and West. With a rare combination of scientific rigor, poetic appreciation, and spiritual insight, *Contemplative Inquiry* will enrich the lives of all those who read it and even more so those who put its wise counsel into practice."

B. ALLAN WALLACE
author of *The Attention Revolution: Unlocking the Power of the Focused Mind*

The great turn needed to reverse problems like climate change and the growing gap between rich and poor is none other than the one that we can accomplish in our own ways of thinking and living together. I believe much of the discouragement and fear that pervades our world today comes from not seeing this connection between the outer circumstances of our world and our inner landscape. Once we have seen it, however, our core work becomes clear. We must bring our outer and inner change strategies into ever greater alignment. Arthur Zajonc is one of the our best guides in the new art of traversing the narrowing gulf between science, consciousness, and social change. This beautiful book embodies the best in his writing. He gives us simple and clear expositions of subtle concepts, touching evocations of timeless insights, and, above all meditative exercises that each of us can start practicing whenever we are ready.

PETER SENGE
author of *The Fifth Discipline: The Art and Practice of the Learning Organization.*